CHRISTOLOGY AND TRANSITION IN THE THEOLOGY OF EDWIN LEWIS

Stephen A. Seamands

Associate Professor of Christian Doctrine
Asbury Theological Seminary

UNIVERSITY
PRESS OF
AMERICA

Lanham • New York • London

British Cataloging in Publication Information Available

Library of Congress Cataloging-in-Publication Data

Seamands, Stephen A., 1949-
  Christology and transition in the theology of
Edwin Lewis.

  Bibliography: p.
  Includes index.
  1. Jesus Christ—History of doctrines—20th century.
2. Lewis, Edwin, 1881-   . I. Title.
BT198.S38   1987   232'.092'4   87-8255
ISBN 0-8191-6381-3 (alk. paper)
ISBN 0-8191-6382-1 (pbk. : alk. paper)

All University Press of America books are produced on acid-free
paper which exceeds the minimum standards set by the National
Historical Publication and Records Commission.

Dedication

To my father, David Seamands, through whose life and ministry I first felt the influence of Edwin Lewis, and whose love and admiration for his great teacher of theology inspired me to study about him.

TABLE OF CONTENTS

PREFACE

If Methodists are ever going to understand and appropriate their theological tradition, it is essential that they become better acquainted not only with the theology of John Wesley, but also with the contributions of their major theological figures since Wesley. That, however, is difficult when there are so few published studies available which deal with those figures. This study, then, is an attempt to fill a part of what is still a very large gap by focusing upon one of those figures, Edwin Lewis, a twentieth century Methodist theologian. As such it is the first published work exclusively devoted to Lewis and apart from some minor editorial changes represents my doctoral dissertation submitted to the graduate school of Drew University in the spring of 1983.

There is, of course, much more that needs to be written about Edwin Lewis. His theology as a whole, his relationship to the earlier theologians of Drew, his influence as a teacher-at-large to the Methodist Church and to generations of students at Drew, his place in the larger theological scene -- all these, though touched upon in this study, deserve careful attention in themselves. But this work should at least serve as a first step in facilitating understanding and further study of this significant Methodist theologian, and hence contribute to our knowledge of Methodist theology as a whole.

I would particularly like to express my gratitude to Kenneth Rowe, my chief dissertation advisor, for all his encouragement and helpful suggestions in relation to this study. I would also like to thank Abingdon Press and Mrs. Faulkner Lewis for permission to quote from the writings of Edwin Lewis. Above all I would like to thank my wife Carol, and my four children, Matthew, Jason, Joseph, and Stephanie for their love, encouragement, and sacrifice, without which this work would have never been completed.

INTRODUCTION

Edwin Lewis, who taught systematic theology at Drew from 1916 to 1951, deserves an important place in any discussion of twentieth century American Methodist theology, as well as twentieth century American theology in general. Through his numerous writings he was one of the first to introduce neo-orthodox theology to America, and through his skill as a teacher and lecturer he was instrumental in shaping a whole generation of Methodist pastors and theologians.

However, apart from a few introductory articles,[1] several dissertations where Lewis is studied along with one or more other theologians,[2] and one dissertation devoted to his theodicy,[3] very little serious attention has been given to the unique manner in which his theology developed, or to his theological contribution itself. William Lewis is therefore correct in his observation that "the full significance of the contribution of Edwin Lewis to the theology of American Methodism is largely unexplored."[4] Shortly after Lewis' death in 1959, Carl Michalson,[5] his student and successor at Drew, spoke of several "myths" about his predecessor that needed to be put to rest, but unfortunately, because of the lack of sufficient research those myths still linger on.

It is thus the purpose of this study to further our knowledge of Edwin Lewis' theology and his theological development, and to do so by examining one major aspect of his theology, namely, his Christology.

This approach will prove fruitful for several reasons. First, regardless of the period of his theological development, Christology is always at the center of Lewis' thought. His first major work, <u>Jesus Christ and the Human Quest</u>,[6] was completely devoted to this crucial area of theology and is indicative of the centrality of Christology in all his theological endeavors throughout his long career. As John Sims observes, Christology is "the interpretive key to Lewis' understanding of the Christian revelation."[7] Moreover, because it is so interrelated with his understanding of all other major Christian doctrines, analyzing his Christology can also serve as an introduction to his theology as a whole.

xi

Second, by analyzing Lewis' Christology, and particularly the changes in the way it was formulated, we can also analyze that for which Edwin Lewis is probably best remembered: his so-called theological "conversion" or transition. Actually there are two transitions in Lewis' theology which must be considered, a major one and a minor one. The first transition, the major one, which Lewis characterized as a shift "from philosophy to revelation,"[8] is the transition for which Lewis became famous, and the one that has received almost all the attention. But there is also a second transition, minor when compared to the first, yet significant nonetheless, a transition which can be described as "from monism to dualism." A careful examination of Lewis' Christology in the light of these transitions themselves, and help us to understand their causes, nature, and extent.

Third, by analyzing Lewis' Christology and particularly the reactions which it provoked both within Methodism and without, we can gain a better understanding of Methodist theology during this period, as well as American theology in general. This was a time of theological unrest and upheaval so that the changes which took place in Lewis' thinking are reflective of changes which were taking place in American theology as a whole. A careful study of Lewis should thus help us to understand why there was a growing dissatisfaction with theological liberalism, and why the reaction against it took the particular form it did.

Our investigation will proceed chronologically. At each stage of Lewis' theological development we will examine his approach to theology, and then proceed to describe the Christology which followed from that approach. Major attention will also be given to the transitions which, of course, resulted in changes in his approach.

We will primarily be focusing on Lewis' numerous published writings.[9] But in addition to these we will be using several other sources. First, the Edwin Lewis Collection in Rose Memorial Library at Drew University, which consists mostly of letters written to and from Lewis. Second, the Harold Paul Sloan Papers in the Methodist Archives on the Drew campus which contain correspondence between Sloan and Lewis. And finally, typewritten class notes of lectures by Edwin Lewis taken by two students in courses such as "Christian Theology," "The Doctrine of the Incarnation," and "The Theology of the Atonement." Along with his published materials, these additional sources will prove helpful in analyzing Lewis' Christology and the transitions in his thought.

NOTES TO INTRODUCTION

1. Charley D. Hardwick, "Edwin Lewis: Introductory and Critical Remarks," <u>Drew Gateway</u> 33 (Winter 1963): 91-104; William J. McCutcheon, "American Methodist Thought and Theology, 1919-1960," in <u>History of American Methodism</u>, vol. 3, Emory S. Bucke, ed. (Nashville: Abingdon Press, 1964), pp. 304-315; John A. Sims, "Revelation and Apologetic in the Theology of Edwin Lewis," <u>Drew Gateway</u> 51 (Spring 1981): 1-33; David W. Soper, <u>Major Voices in American Theology</u> (Philadelphia: Westminster Press, 1953), pp. 15-36.

2. Marvin Green, "Contemporary Theories of Evil. An Ethical View: Reinhold Niebuhr; A Philosophical View: E.S. Brightman; A Theological View: Edwin Lewis," Ph.D. dissertation, Drew University, 1945; S. Jameson Jones, Jr., "Three Representative Leaders in Contemporary American Methodist Theology," Ph.D. dissertation, Vanderbilt University, 1965; John A. Sims, "The Problem of Knowledge in the Apolegetic Concerns of Edwin Lewis and Edward John Carnell," Ph.D. dissertation, Florida State University, 1975.

3. Deane L. Shaffer, "The Theodicy of Edwin Lewis," Th.D. dissertation, Southern Baptist Theological Seminary, 1959.

4. William B. Lewis, "The Role of Harold Paul Sloan and the Methodist League for Faith and Life in the Fundamentalist Modernist Controversy of the Methodist Episcopal Church," Ph.D. dissertation, Vanderbilt University, 1963, pp. 270-271.

5. Carl Michalson, "The Edwin Lewis Myth," <u>Christian Century</u> 77 (24 February 1960): 217-219.

6. Edwin Lewis, <u>Jesus Christ and the Human Quest; Suggestions Toward a Philosophy of the Person and Work of Christ</u> (New York: Abingdon Press, 1924).

7. Sims, "The Problem of Knowledge in the Apologetic Concerns of Edwin Lewis and Edward John Carnell," p. 3. See also p. 170.

8. Edwin Lewis, "From Philosophy to Revelation,"
    <u>Christian Century</u> 56 (14 June 1939): 762-764.

9. See John Caldwell, <u>Edwin Lewis: An Enumerative</u>
    <u>Bibliography</u> (Madison,   New   Jersey: Drew
    University, 1960).

CHAPTER I

THE HUMAN CHRIST

Lewis' Apologetic Concern

"He wanted the skeptics to hear what he had to say, and he knew they could be persuaded to listen only on their own terms."[1] With these words David Soper aptly describes the apologetic concern which runs throughout the early writings of Edwin Lewis. Above all, he wanted to relate the Christian faith to the modern mind.

Lewis himself explicitly states this again and again. For example, in A Manual of Christian Beliefs, he speaks about the need "to rehabilitate Christianity from the modern point of view."[2] And in Jesus Christ and the Human Quest he indicates his purpose is to give both the modern mind and the truths of historic Christianity their rightful place since the two are not necessarily opposed to each other.[3] He even maintains that this is the primary task of a teacher of theology: "In a word, he will seek to make the Christian faith intelligible to men of the twentieth century . . ."[4]

Of course, Edwin Lewis was not the only theologian of this period who was convinced this was necessary. Rather, his concern to relate the Christian faith to the modern mind was shared by virtually all the major American theologians during this era when theological liberalism was at its height.

It was, in fact, out of this concern that liberalism arose in the first place. At the turn of the century, men such as Henry Churchill King[5] had argued that a reconstruction in theology was necessary not primarily because of the inherent weaknesses of traditional theology, but because of the demand that the living faith come to terms with the modern world. The gradual acceptance of the theory of evolution in the natural sciences, the historical-critical method in biblical interpretation, and the trend toward pantheism in philosophy all combined to present a challenge to traditional orthodoxy that could not be ignored. Thus liberalism arose, as Kenneth Cauthen suggests, "to adjust the ancient faith to the modern world."[6] Or as Harry Emerson Fosdick often stated, to make it possible to be "both an intelligent modern and a serious Christian."[7]

1

Within American Methodism there was at first considerable resistance to the movement, but by the end of World War I liberal theology had become dominant and was being espoused in one form or another[8] by every major Methodist theologian except one.[9] The early writings of Edwin Lewis, then, reflect this common concern of theological liberalism. To use Soper's words again, they grew out of "his desire to make the gospel acceptable to the strongest of the skeptics, and on their own ground."[10]

Lewis was convinced that only by accomodating its theological expression to the thought forms of the day could the Christian faith be preserved and perpetuated. Historically, he maintained, whenever theology had failed to do this it had "always involved disaster."[11] As an example, Lewis cited the failure of the reformation theologians to take Erasmus and the humanists seriously enough.[12] After summarizing what took place he concluded, "He misreads history who thinks that that was a good thing. It was <u>not</u> a good thing, any more than it would be a good thing today for theology to ignore 'the New Learning.' <u>But it won't!</u>"[13]

The Commitment to Philosophy

Lewis, then, was committed to the task of bringing the evangelical faith and the modern mind together. He was also committed to a particular method in carrying out that task. Later as he reflected upon <u>Jesus Christ and the Human Quest</u>, the most significant and representative expression of his early theology, Lewis described it as an attempt "to preserve the great evangelical emphases on a philosophical basis arrived at in the first place with no least reference [sic] to Christianity itself."[14] Thus the foundation of his early theology was philosophy. He was convinced that by presenting the truths of Christianity within the framework of a currently accepted philosophical position the faith could be made more credible to many.

A good example of his methodology at work is found in "The Divine Triunity,"[15] an article which appeared in the <u>Methodist Review</u> in 1918. Here Lewis is dealing with a doctrine which many moderns find difficult and incomprehensible: the doctrine of the Trinity. Recognizing this, Lewis cites R.C. Moberly's statement that "no one has yet succeeded in formulating a Christian metaphysic, based on orthodox Trinitarianism, which this age can accept."[16] He then attempts to formulate just such a metaphysic.

First, he outlines the "data" of the doctrine. Trinitarianism is necessary, he maintains, because of the nature of God's self-revelation, the teaching of the New Testament, and the character of Christian experience. Then Lewis makes this significant statement:

> But the data for the Trinitarian doctrine are found not only in the more distinctive Christian facts which have been suggested, but also in certain philosophical considerations. When a Christian fact and a philosophical necessity appear to point in the same direction, the mind receives increased assurance.[17]

The "philosophical necessity" which Lewis has in mind is the nature of perfect personality; and this becomes the basis for his construction of the doctrine of the Trinity. Assuming that God is one perfect personality, and that human beings are made in his image, we can work back from the nature of humanity to the nature of divinity.

Beginning then on the human level, we can show that perfect personality cannot exist in the individual person; rather, it exists as a complex of individual persons, each incomplete in themselves but finding their completeness in their shared life and experience. If this is therefore the case on the human level, although in an imperfect way, can we not infer that it must also be the case on the divine level in a perfect way? On this basis, then, we can reaffirm the doctrine of the Trinity and will have "made real progress toward a metaphysic of the kind desired."[18]

The Influence of Pringle-Pattison

Thus by stressing their compatibility with the current assumptions of philosophy Lewis sought to make the truths of Christianity credible to the modern mind. The basis of his construction of the doctrine of the Trinity -- the nature of perfect personality -- also introduces us to the particular philosophy upon which Lewis built his early theology: personal idealism.

In this regard, Lewis had been influenced by

Borden Parker Bowne,[19] and particularly his reading of Andrew Seth Pringle-Pattison's[20] The Idea of God in the Light of Recent Philosophy,[21] the Gifford Lectures of 1912-1913. Regarding the impact of that work upon him he later wrote:

> The book said just the things I had long been searching for. It seemed to me to take the best in Kant, the best in Hegel, the best in Lotze, and the best of the so-called British idealists, and combine them in a view of remarkable coherence and strength. The book spoke to me (and for me) as few books have ever done.[22]

It is important, then, to summarize the essential content of Pringle-Pattison's book in order to understand how Lewis formulated his early theology.

Pringle-Pattison is critical of the philosophy of naturalism because it so emphasizes the continuity between humanity and nature that it minimizes and sometimes even denies their differences. Everyone recognizes that there is continuity within the order of nature, but it is a mistake to so emphasize this aspect that we lose sight of other equally important aspects of nature such as the emergence of significant differences within various levels.

It is also a mistake to limit our description of the higher levels of nature only to categories applicable to the lower levels. Categories which are appropriate for describing inorganic matter are sometimes inadequate for describing organic matter; human beings will demand categories which are not applicable to insects. Naturalism, i.e. "the lower naturalism," as Pringle-Pattison calls it, wants to deny the existence of these differences. The result is a misuse of the principle of continuity and "the reduction of all nature's facts to the dead level of a single type."[23]

Pringle-Pattison, on the other hand, advocates a "higher naturalism" which is opposed to this process of "levelling down," and which stresses both continuity and divergence as "twin aspects of the cosmic history."[24] Whereas the "lower natuaralism" wants to "merge man in the infra-human nature from which he draws his nature,"[25] the "higher naturalism" interprets nature and the universe in the light of humanity. Thus

4

human experience, in all its reaches, reflects and reveals the nature of reality. In words which express the dominate theme of the book[26] Pringle-Pattison declares:

> Man is organic to the world . . . the world is not complete without him. The intelligent being is, as it were, the organ through which the universe beholds and enjoys itself.[27]

This applies, first of all, to his knowledge of the world. Because each human being is "from beginning to end, even qua knower, a member and, as it were an organ of the universe, knowledge will appear to us in a more natural light and we shall not be tempted to open this miraculous chasm between the knower and the realities which he knows."[28] Understood in this way, the epistemological problem fades away. We can assume with the pragmatists that things are as they are experienced, and with the neorealists that knowledge is a direct relation between the knower and the reality known.[29]

Moreover, what holds true in the realm of "primary qualities," i.e. a human being's knowledge of the external world, also holds true in the realm of "secondary qualities" such as the ability to perceive beauty, and the capacity for poetic imagination. The fact that humans, the knowers within the system which they know, possess these capabilities suggests to us that they do in fact exist. These aesthetic powers have developed "as an instrument of nature's purpose of self-revelation."[30] They are therefore not to be looked upon as secondary qualities nor as "subjective imaginings" for they "give us a deeper truth than ordinary vision, just as the more developed eye or ear carries us farther into nature's refinements and beauties."[31]

Pringle-Pattison believed this to be true particularly with regard to the poetic imagination which he considered to be one of the chief gateways to reality. He quotes with approval Wordsworth's description of poetry as "the breath and finer spirit of all knowledge," and Yeats' assertion that "whatever of philosophy has been made poetry is alone permanent."[32] The poet, he concludes, "is a revealer; he teaches us to see, and what he shows us is really in the facts. It is not put into them, but elicited from

5

them by his intenser sympathy."[33]

Following his discussion of the aesthetic nature of human beings Pringle-Pattison turns to their moral and ethical nature. This too is not merely subjective, but is a trustworthy indicator of the nature of reality. He is therefore critical of the positivism of Comte and similar such philosophies for introducing an unnecessary dualism between nature and humanity by conceiving of nature in a purely mechanical way, and only attributing to humanity a moral and ethical nature. From the standpoint of positivism, nature and humankind are therefore not looked upon as parts of the same whole. Humanity's ethical nature appears in the universe "like a moral Melchizadek without ancestry,"[34] thus bringing into existence something which did not exist before.

According to Pringle-Pattison, however, such a dualism is not necessary. Man is rooted in nature; he does not, therefore,

> . . . step outside of his universal life when he develops the qualities of a moral being; . . . Man is the child of nature, and it is on the basis of natural impulses and in commerce with the system of external things, that his ethical being is built up. The characteristics of the ethical life must be taken, therefore, as contributing to determine the nature of the system in which we live. Nay, according to the interpretation . . . the ethical predicates must carry us nearer to a true definition of the ultimate life in which we live than the categories which suffice to describe, for example, the environmental conditions of our experience.[35]

Thus a human being's moral consciousness, feeling for values, search for the ideal -- these are the most real things in the world. Consequently those ranges of our experience such as religion, which are based upon it, "instead of being treated as a cloud-cuckoo-land of subjective fancy, may reasonably be accepted as the best interpreters we have of the nature of reality."[36]

But from whence does a human being's moral consciousness originate? Human beings do not create it any more than they create themselves; they only

Christ?" The answer, he says, depends on how one approaches the question. In determining our approach, therefore, a distinction must be made between "Christ as object of living faith and Christ as subject of ordered thought."[68] If we approach the question from the standpoint of the latter we will be "confronted with a collection of answers that would be simply chaotic."[69] If, however, we approach the question from the standpoint of the former, we immediately find ourselves "dealing with something definite and tangible. There is not a man of our representative group but would answer, 'The place of complete moral and spiritual lordship.'"[70]

This, then, is the common element among all who have a Christian attitude toward Christ: they assign to him "complete moral worth"; they recognize that he is the answer to their moral, spiritual and social needs; they find in him the fulfillment of that purpose for which they were created.[71] What is important to note here is that Lewis has located the "common element" in Christianity not in something outside of humanity, but in human nature itself. If religion is to have a permanent basis, he maintains, it must be rooted here. The moment it looks to anything other than human nature, "to custom, to an institution, to a book, to external authority of any kind whatsoever -- that moment it is shifted to a basis which must eventually crumble."[72] Lewis therefore commends Kant, Schleiermacher, and Hegel[73] in that despite their differences over what constituted the basis of religion, they all rightly rooted it in elemental human nature.

As for Lewis himself, that aspect of human nature which serves as the basis of religion, he characterizes broadly as "end-seeking activity."[74] This end-seeking activity consists of three different elements: individuality, sociality, and ideality. Individuality refers to that original element in each human being which distinguishes persons from each other. Sociality, on the other hand, means that no one lives in total isolation from others, but that we are all part of a larger social whole. These two elements in end-seeking activity, individuality and sociality, are to be held in balance. As Lewis states,

> The facts in the case require us to
> believe that there is in the individual a
> potential independence and a certain

pecularity of selfhood, but that potentially independent individual is inextricably embosomed in the social milieu.[75]

Ideality suggests that deep within each human being there is a sense of a beyond, of the supernatural, of God. Conscience confirms this, and attests to the fact that humans feel obligated to that "beyond" and vest it with absolute moral authority. Man, therefore, is "meant for God, and short of God he is not wholly man."[76]

Growing out of these three elements of end-seeking activity is the demand for an end of absolute worth or value which when sought after and found will result in the realization and satisfaction of all end-seeking activity. Lewis sees the "facts of life" and the world of things as existing to assist humans in realizing this absolute end.[77] For him that end is not pleasure or utility or blessedness; rather, "that one thing to which every single fact and circumstance of life may contribute is moral character in personality."[78] He therefore concludes his discussion of the human quest by stating that human beings are constituted for moral goodness. This is the one thing for which they exist,[79] and the world around them "provides the necessary conditions of its realization."[80]

The Work of Christ

Christ's moral achievement

Having thus described the end-seeking nature of humanity, and the need for an end of absolute worth, the stage has been set for the work of Christ. It is Jesus Christ who both fully realizes and reveals the absolute end for which human beings were created. "He achieved moral goodness without a flaw, and his achievement becomes at the same time a revelation of the nature of God and of the supreme purpose of God in the world."[81]

Lewis emphasizes that the work of Christ was in fact an achievement. He is therefore critical of Christologies which, by bringing to the study of his moral experience "a prior conception of his person," have made his achievement of perfect moral goodness "a foregone conclusion."[82] Thus it is not because of what he brought into the world that we call Jesus "Lord"; it is because of what he accomplished after he was here.[83]

14

His achievement then was real. It was "personal, not mechanical"; he did not function as "a moral automaton."[84] This is the problem with traditional Christology: it has "taken the human meaning and human hope out of Christ's great achievement"[85] by presenting him as less than fully human.

Christ, however, was fully human. His moral achievement was that of a human being who was in no way different from other humans. The temptations he faced were real -- so was his possibility of moral failure. Only if this is the case will what he did have any bearing on our situation. It is best, therefore, to approach the work of Christ as Mark the gospel writer does -- by beginning with his baptism and temptation. Granted that in the opening words of his gospel Mark does attribute to Jesus the title "Son of God"; but this expression has several meanings, and it is evident as one reads on in the gospel that he meant it to be "not a metaphysical but a moral title."[86]

Thus for Lewis it is Christ's moral achievement which both determines and defines his divinity:

> . . . it is precisely on his moral excellence that the question of his Lordship, his Sonship, and his Saviorhood is dependent today for an increasing number of men . . . If there has ever lived a man who, not merely in personal intention but in the whole reach of his life, inner and outer, has consistently, not occasionally -- we can all do that -- maintained at the full level of the ought for love's sake, there was a man whose achievement was so far forth a divine achievement . . . In such a man, God is manifest in the flesh.
> This is the claim that we make for Jesus Christ. He was the Son of God with power by virtue of his moral achievement.[87]

But Christ's moral achievement was perfect not only in relation to God; it was also perfect in relation to humanity. As he realized and revealed perfect sonship, so did he realize and reveal perfect brotherhood.

In analyzing this aspect of his moral achievement, Lewis discusses three overarching principles which guided Jesus in his relationships with others. The first is the absolute worth of persons. Jesus placed persons above institutions, customs, and laws. He did so because he saw each person as a child of God. Thus "the modern philosophy which makes personality the ultimate form of being and therefore the supreme category of thought and action has unqualified support in everything Jesus ever said and did."[88] A second guiding principle in Christ's relations with others was social obligation. Believing as he did that the welfare of all depended on his fidelity to his vocation, he never spoke or acted without having others in mind. Above all, Jesus was guided by a third principle: sacrificial love. Others have proclaimed the absolute worth of persons and the social obligation, but Jesus alone was able to put these principles into practice. He could do so because his life was governed by perfect love. It is his supremacy at this point which "makes the difference between Jesus as a Wise Man and Jesus as the world's Savior."[89]

The Redemptional Requirement

At this point in his discussion of the work of Christ, Lewis introduces the problem of sin. Sin, he stresses, is real and tangible; it creates a moral situation that cannot be ignored or passed over lightly. Hence although Christ's moral achievement of sonship and brotherhood was a perfect achievement, by itself it is inadequate to meet the total need of humanity. The nature and extent of human sin necessitates more.

In analyzing the nature of sin Lewis states that men and women "acquire and cultivate sinful dispositions, and manifest them in deeds of like character."[90] Consequently sin consists of two basic elements: disposition and deed. The sinful disposition grows out of the failure to bring desire under control of the absolute end. The sinful deed not only includes wrong actions but wrong attitudes as well. Knowledge, will, and conscience also play a part in sin; it has social ramifications which further increase its tragic effects. But above all it is the moral situation it creates in humanity which concerns Lewis:

> Human nature is out of gear. It is the seat of an internal dualism. The same man in the same situation both would and would not. He does as he does, knowing all the while

that he will hate himself for doing it. He is morally disorganized.[91]

In light of this, salvation "cannot be accomplished by the mere presentation of the ideal Perfect Sonship and Brotherhood."[92] The problem of sin, both as disposition and deed, must be dealt with. Something must be done to blot out the sinful deeds that have been committed and to break the dominion of the sinful disposition so that similar deeds will not necessarily be committed in the future.

This leads, then, to a discussion of the nature of redemption, or as Lewis calls it, "the redemptional requirement."[93] He begins by noting that much harm has been done in the past by reading into the word "redemption" much that is not there.[94] Rather than repeating this error, it is thus better to look upon redemption simply as a metaphor for deliverance, and to conceive of it in a twofold manner. There is "that *from* whose control he [humanity] needs to be delivered, and there is that *unto* whose control he needs to be delivered."[95] (italics mine).

Following a brief survey of how women and men have typically sought redemption, Lewis proceeds to describe the Christian method under five headings: revelation, forgiveness, empowerment, redemptive service, and permanence.

Revelation and forgiveness

Concerning the first of these, revelation, he states that "the necessary basis of an adequate message of redemption is a knowledge of the conditions out of which the very need of redemption arises."[96] In his perfect sonship, realized and revealed through his total person -- both words and actions --Jesus Christ meets this "redemptional requirement," for by his perfect sonship he reveals to us that God is Father.

Never before had humans seen the Father. In Jesus, however, they saw the Son, and "from the Sonship they inferred the Fatherhood."[97] As Father, God desires from each human being joyful obedience and uninterrupted fellowship. These are the two "hallmarks of the filial spirit,"[98] and they in turn define the nature of Christian redemption: "the establishing of the filial relation, or man's realization of sonship to God."[99] They also shed light upon the nature of sin:

17

it is anything which is unfilial and unfraternal; it is the disobedience of a child.

The nature of sin, in turn, defines the nature of forgiveness, the second element in redemption. Forgiveness is conceived not as a verdict of innocence or a legal fiction; rather, it is "the Father's declaration that the child being no longer wayward and rebellious, but loyal and obedient, . . . is restored to favor and accorded all the privileges of sonship."[100]

But upon what is this forgiveness based? How can we be certain that such a change in relations does in fact take place? Lewis answers: because we believe in Jesus Christ. If Christ forgave men's and women's sins, can the Father do less? Thus it is upon "the identity in moral quality and therefore in moral authority between the Son and the Father,"[101] that the ultimate basis of forgiveness rests.

This, however, raises a question: if this is the basis of forgiveness, why was the cross of Christ necessary? Why the repeated New Testament emphasis on the death of Christ in relation to the forgiveness of sins? The answer, according to Lewis, lies in the nature of repentance. We know that "repentance is the condition to forgiveness, but what is the condition to repentance?"[102] he asks. The answer then follows: the condition for a complete repentance is "a clear comprehension of the nature of fault."[103]

God's problem then is how to induce in his wayward children an adequate repentance. His answer lies in the death of his Son which made atonement by revealing the nature of sin for both God and humanity thus making an adequate repentance possible. As Lewis explains it,

> Christ atoned for sin because he bore it to the point of dying for it, and the sin that broke the heart of such a One as he, did, in the very moment of its triumph, sound its own death knell, for it therein stood self-revealed. In the moral history of humanity there is needed such a deed as shall by its very nature guarantee the final defeat of sin. Such a deed was Calvary, and all that of which it was the inevitable sequence. The world for which Christ died simply cannot be lost. He has saved it, not by bearing

some calculated equivalent of what it deserved, not by satisfying the inexorable demand of an eternal law, but by suffering and dying in loyalty to his great vocation to show men God by being himself God's Perfect Son. A Christian repentance is, therefore, a repentance made in view of Jesus Christ and all that he was and did and desired men to do and to become.[104]

There may be some, however, who question whether this view does away with the objective element in the atonement. Lewis responds that this depends entirely upon how objectivity is understood. If by objectivity we mean that Christ was somehow punished by God the exact penalty for human sin, or that through his death the moral law of God was displayed, then it is best to "frankly surrender" the idea without apology.[105] On the other hand objectivity can simply be taken to mean:

> He suffered for me. My sin slew him.
> He is my Sin-offering. For me he bore the
> shameful cross. Through him I find God.
> Because of him I am forgiven.[106]

Empowerment

Having thus indicated how the work of Christ meets the need of humankind for knowledge and forgiveness, Lewis turns to the third redemptional requirement: empowerment. The Christian claim is that the same Christ who reveals and atones also empowers. This power, however, is "not some tangible entity that falls upon a man from without as rain falls upon the thirsty ground";[107] rather it is power that has its source within the human heart itself. It therefore comes upon men and women "in the only way in which such power can come -- by the arousing of a great emotion."[108]

Thus there are certain necessary psychological conditions which when met, cause the power within human beings to be released. Lewis mentions three: a sense of indebtedness, a change in attention, and creative love.

By the first of these, a sense of indebtedness, Lewis has in mind the profound awareness that comes upon the believer that "what Christ did, he did for me." When a person -- sincerely not perfunctorily -- recognizes this, that sense of indebtedness becomes "focused into a personal feeling of overwhelming intensity."[109]

The second condition necessary for empowerment, a change in attention, involves the new awareness that one's sins are not committed against an impersonal moral law, but against a person. Seen in this way our sins become a matter of "disloyalty to a Personal Friend whose love never fails us although we have failed him."[110] Growing out of this changed attention is the third condition which creates empowerment: creative love. What we could never do under the constraint of the law, we find ourselves able to do when compelled by love. "What Law cannot do, Love can do -- it can supply the adequate motive."[111]

Lewis thus describes the process of empowerment in psychological terms. But by doing so he does not want to imply that it can be totally explained in this way; it is, he insists, a distinctive religious experience as well. Thus it is "a divine self-impartation,"[112] and will "always outstrip our attempted psychology of it."[113] Yet in stressing its religious dimension we must not make the mistake of taking spatial terms such as "drawing near" or "coming down from above" literally. "The 'beyond' is really 'within.' God is wherever man is. The law of the man's life is the law of God himself."[114]

Redemptive service

The fourth element in the redemptive process, redemptive service, is required because sin is social as well as individual. We have sinned not only against the Father but against the other members of the household as well. Redemption, therefore, must be social too. It is this aspect of the Christian redemption which makes it "the most profoundly ethical process the world has ever known."[115] This ethical process consists of three elements: direct restitution, social devotion, and the motivation of love.

Direct restitution means that forgiven sinners feel obligated to right their wrongs. Not that restitution will ever be absolute, neither will it issue out of a need to earn our salvation or to pay back God for what He has done, but nevertheless, ". . . he who is content not to do all he could do to 'make right' where he has been consciously at fault has

20

certainly not yet read the mind of Christ."[116]

Social devotion arises when the principle of restitution is lifted out of the realm of the particular and applied to the realm of the universal. We may, in fact, be able to do little by way of direct reparation for our sins; but when we realize that a sin against one human being is a sin against the entire human race, then there is opened up for us a limitless number of possibilities for indirect reparation. Thus,

> The service of Humanity becomes the correlate of the true interpretation of Calvary. Such are the interrelations of human life . . . that there are no limits discernible to the healing influences issuing from the service of love rendered to a common humanity in the name of Jesus Christ.[117]

Underlying all true redemptive service is the motive of love for Christ. Because Christians acknowledge that Christ is their redeemer, they love him. In loving him, they also love his cause. Since his cause embraces the entire human race, they are therefore committed to working with him to the end that all might acknowledge his Lordship.

Everlastingness

The fifth redemptional requirement, everlastingness, concerns the future. Will the redemption offered in Christ ever be superseded or become outmoded? Perfect and complete for men and women today, will it continue to be the same tomorrow? Lewis emphasizes that the achievement of Christ carries with it the guarantee of permanence and unequivocally affirms the finality of Christ:

> We claim for the Christian way not only that it is the best that is known but that it is the best that can be conceived. We claim for Jesus Christ not that he is merely the greatest of Prophets and the greatest of Teachers, but that he is in a category all by himself -- Incarnate Deity in the sense that he is why things are, the Alpha and Omega of creation . . . Christ is not merely a Redeemer: he is The Redeemer. He is not merely a Son of man and a Son of God: he is Son of Man and Son of God. He is not merely

21

one who speaks for God: he is God speaking. He is not merely one more link in an evolutionary process which began before him and which will some day outgrow him: he _consummates_ the process, in the sense that what now remains to be done is to explicate, appropriate, and make real all that lies implicit in him and his work and his Cause. These are strong statements, and they are made purposely so. No exigencies of apologetic strategy shall lead us to abate one jot or tittle this claim that to Jesus Christ belongs the absolute moral Lordship of the human race forever because in him is the potency to bring every man in his individual, social, and spiritual nature to complete self-fulfillment.[118]

Lewis discusses the implications of such an affirmation. It requires, for example, that Christ be a real historic person and not merely someone with whom we associate certain religious ideas. Then he turns to answer the challenge to Christ's finality on the basis that there may come a time when human nature itself changes. Lewis contends that it is simply wasting time to conjecture about such a situation.

For when we speak of fundamental human nature we are speaking of personality, and if personality is not the ultimate form of being, and therefore the ultimate category of thought, then the possibility of a rational interpretation of experience disappears.[119]

The Person of Christ

The facts

As he begins his consideration of the person of Christ, Lewis notes that up to this point the primary basis for his Christology has been the facts of Scripture, history, and experience. Now however that will change and the discussion will move "almost exclusively in the realm of the speculative."[120] This change though is only natural. Faith seeks understanding; the Christ of living faith leads us to the Christ of ordered thought. The "coordinating function of reason"[121] must be brought to bear upon the facts which form the basis of faith.

Lewis turns then to an examination of the facts related to the person of Christ beginning with the portrait of Christ found in the synoptic gospels. Here he discusses several recent approaches to the gospel materials which have interpreted the facts in a way that evades the problem of Christ's person.

The crudest of these is the approach which flatly denies that Jesus was a historical figure. Such a theory, he maintains, is "not even plausible."[122] In asking us to believe that the apostles and early Christians were willing to suffer as they did for something they knew never actually happened it simply stretches our credulity beyond the breaking point.

Another inadequate approach interprets the synoptics in such a way that Christ is reduced to a mere man. Although we must not deny the right of criticism to reconstruct the gospel materials when the writers have been unduly influenced by the presuppositions of their age, we must also recognize that critics who employ this method have their presuppositions too. Often they have assumed that anything which presupposes the supernatural must automatically be unhistorical. In doing so they have already prejudged the case:

> They want no other than a humanitarian Christ; they believe that the humanitarian was also the historical Christ; and they so employ the method that the Gospel story is made to support the prejudgment. They say in effect: "There could not have been such a Person as Jesus is portrayed to have been."[123]

A third approach to the gospels which evades the problem is one which seeks to interpret Jesus solely in the light of the prevailing apocalyptic of his day. This approach is to be commended in that it seeks to understand Jesus in the light of his own times. Moreover, it is clear that Jesus was influenced by apocalyptic and employed it in his teaching. But the question remains: can the person of Christ be wholly explained by it? This, according to Lewis, is where the approach falls short. It simply cannot adequately account for the unique self-consciousness of Jesus:

> The Strong Son of God of Mark's Gospel a deluded visionary -- "a sorry figure"! The

Preacher of "The Sermon on the Mount" an
impractical dreamer laying down the rules as
to how his disciples should act during the
few days or weeks or months -- he didn't know
how long -- before the coming of the Kingdom
would abrogate them all! . . . Yes, it evades
the problem, but what shall we do with the
problem it leaves us with -- the problem of a
gross misapprehension by the Savior of his
real position and the problem of a gross
misrepresentation of him by those who have
told us his story.[124]

A fourth way of evading the problem -- and perhaps
the most serious of all -- is to uncritically accept
the so-called orthodox solution that has been handed
down to us. What we must never forget is that
originally this solution was only set forth after a
serious consideration and grappling with the issues
involved. Before we accept it, then, we need to
struggle with the issues ourselves. This orthodox
solution can be summed up in the following manner:

In Jesus Christ we have One Person into
the basal condition of whose life there
entered at one and the same time, and without
confusion or division, the divine nature and
the human nature.[125]

Thus one of the crucial questions facing contemporary
theology is this: Can we distinguish between the truth
of this statement and the statement itself; and can we
state this truth as forcefully and powerfully in our
day as those who originally formulated the statement
did in theirs?[126]

As to his own approach to the synoptics, Lewis
affirms their substantial reliability: "The Portrait
may not be a photograph, but it is incredible that the
lineaments here portrayed are not those of a living
Subject."[127]

He then turns to the second body of facts related
to the person of Christ: the apostolic consciousness
found in the epistles and the gospel of John. The
crucial question here does not concern the so-called
inconsistencies between the picture of Christ found in
the epistles and the picture found in the synoptic
gospels. As far as Lewis is concerned, the two are in
substantial agreement with each other. The crucial

question concerns "the validity of the apostolic interpretation."[128]

Lewis himself accepts that interpretation as valid, emphasizing that it is based not on "complete identity of language and thought-forms,"[129] but on a common spiritual reality all had experienced. When we analyze all their various descriptions of that reality, what do we find?

We find the belief that in Jesus Christ the very God tabernacled in the flesh, that the presence in the world of such a Person had a universal significance, that he was somehow necessary to God and yet equally necessary to mankind, and that he did what he did in order that through him men might have life and might have it more abundantly.[130]

The same experience of the transforming power of Christ and the belief in his redemptive significance for all humanity also meets us in the two other bodies of facts related to the person of Christ, i.e. the course of Christian history and the experience of individual Christians. Taken together with the synoptic gospels and the apostolic consciousness these four bodies of facts contain the materials necessary for the construction of a doctrine of the person of Christ.

The kenotic theory

Before actually beginning to construct his own doctrine, however, Lewis deals with a theory which many have found useful in solving the problem of the person of Christ, viz., the kenotic theory. This theory which was advanced to explain the mystery of how God became a human being states that God became human through an act of self-emptying or kenosis.[131] The Son, being truly God, renounced the divine estate and the divine mode of existence and assumed the human estate and the human mode of existence without at any time, however, ceasing to be God.[132]

Lewis recognizes the theory has a number of strengths. Its antiquity, its compatability with the doctrine of the virgin birth, its dramatic intensity, its stress on the cost of redemption, its emotional appeal, and its preachability[133] all stand in its favor. However he also finds the kenotic theory riddled with difficulties and rejects it for a number of reasons. Essentially they can be reduced to two.

First, "kenoticism involves an impossible disruption of the being of God."[134] If God exists as three self-conscious persons, and if for any reason one of those persons became unconscious, as must have been the case in the early stages of the incarnation as presented in kenoticism, then it stands to reason that God would cease to exist. "On Kenotic presuppositions, the necessarily Triune God became in effect Biune -- but how could he?"[135] This impossible disruption of God's being is further evidenced by the "wholly unintelligible" kenotic notion that the Eternal Mind can 'forget.'"[136]

Lewis also rejects the kenotic theory because he understands the incarnation as a progressive event and the divinity of Christ in terms of his ever-increasing God-consciousness. So he states:

> It is precisely in the unique degree of that process that we find the real ground of our Lord's supernaturalness. We make the incarnation progressive, and it is only as it is progressive that it is intelligible. It cannot be confined to any one moment, or be identified with any one event.[137]

This is precisely the problem with the kenotic theory. It confines the incarnation exclusively to one moment and one event: the virgin birth of Christ. By making that one event "absolutely determinative of the later personality and its unique self-consciousness,"[138] it tends to neglect the need for growth, development, and continuous divine activity in the life of Jesus. As a result, it destroys his great moral achievement.

In rejecting the kenotic theory, however, Lewis does not want to be misunderstood. In no way is he implying that he wants to sever the unique connection between God and Christ. Lewis is not a Unitarian and he does not want to be mistaken as one. Jesus Christ is more than a good man or a great teacher. Christianity is a religion of redemption and it is so because God was in Christ. He therefore states categorically, "Any representation of Christianity which eliminates from the work and the Person of Christ the specific activity of the divine cannot do justice to the facts."[139]

Christ, then, not only tells us about God; he is not merely a man peculiarly endowed with God's spirit. What we see in him can only be described as a "Divine Manifestation."[140] This divine manifestation is two-sided: the divine appears as the human, and the human appears as the divine. This does not mean, however, that Christ possessed two consciousnesses or two wills. He had only one consciousness. In describing it Lewis reveals his understanding of the nature of Christ's divinity. It is a consciousness,

> . . . whose content in respect to God's innermost nature, in respect to his purpose for men, in respect to his attitude to sin, in respect to the moral necessities which his own nature creates, is identical with the content of the absolute Divine Consciousness itself . . . In Jesus Christ we meet One who thought as God thought, who acted as God acted, who suffered as God suffered, and who therefore, . . . manifests God, or reveals God, or is the incarnation of God.[141]

Thus Jesus was divine because there was manifested in him an absolute God-consciousness.

This, however, was not merely a human achievement; it was a divine achievement too:

> Not only do we need a special quality in the human instrument through which God manifests himself, but we need also special action -- let us say supernatural action -- on the part of God in his relation to the instrument and in his use of him.[142]

Jesus is thus Son of Man and Son of God, and he is the one because he is the other. Understood in this way, the incarnation reveals to us, once and for all, that "man is essentially kin to God, the law of the uncreated Divine is also the law of the created human."[143]

The humanity of Christ

In the final chapters of <u>Jesus Christ and the Human Quest</u>, Lewis examines the "great historic emphases" -- the full humanity of Christ, his

27

uniqueness, universality, and timelessness -- in an effort to preserve them on the basis of his philosophical position.[144] Since his presentation of Christ's uniqueness, universality, and timelessness is simply a restatement (at times in the exact same words) of the position discussed above[145] it is not necessary to summarize these chapters. However, his conception of the humanity of Christ does merit our consideration.

Here the discussion centers around two subjects: the virgin birth and the sinlessness of Christ. With regards to the virgin birth, Lewis notes that though Matthew, in his account, presents the virgin birth as a fact, Luke's account is ambiguous. He leaves the question of the virgin birth up in the air because he fails to categorically affirm or deny it. This suggests that for Luke, the question of Christ's divinity "was not absolutely dependent upon the manner of his birth" but could be established "by some other avenue than this."[146]

Lewis, then, following what he believes is Luke's intention, seeks to understand the virgin birth in psychological rather than physiological terms. It was something which took place in the mind of Mary,

> who by her prayers and rapturous anticipations of future greatness for her child cooperated with the Spirit of God to bring it to pass that that which was born of her should be called holy, the Son of God.[147]

Understood in this way, Christ's virgin birth thus becomes essentially no different from any human birth. It is governed by the same laws which govern all other births. Only in this way can the full humanity of Christ be maintained.

The same concern for Christ's full humanity also dominates Lewis' discussion of the sinlessness of Christ. "We must save the reality of his humanity, and to do that we must save the reality of his moral trial."[148] His temptations, then, were not in any way artificial, but real. Jesus could have sinned if he had chosen to. His sinlessness, therefore, did not grow "out of an automatic internal coercion, but, rather, in the fact of that divine intimacy which was his . . ."[149]

Thus for Lewis the full humanity of Christ is

critical. Growing out of his philosophical position it is fundamental to his whole Christology. It is from his humanity that we move to his divinity, he argues, and not the other way around.[150] The following statement expresses this central concern of his and fittingly brings our summary of his early Christology to a close:

> It cannot be said too often or with too great emphasis: Jesus Christ so exhibited the characteristic qualities of manhood that it seems never to have occurred to anyone who knew him to doubt his manhood was real. No theory of his Person can be tolerated therefore which is in any wise incompatible with the frankest recognition of his true oneness with men.[151]

A Standard Liberal Christology

What then shall we say in assessing the Christology of the early Lewis? In comparison to the Christologies which were being formulated by other evangelical liberal theologians of this period it is apparent that, in terms of essential content, Lewis' Christology is not particularly novel or unique. S.G. Craig, who wrote a critical review of Jesus Christ and the Human Quest, was quick to point this out:

> It is true, indeed, that Professor Lewis approaches his task from a special point of view but in substance he holds to that conception of Christ and his work that has become traditional in liberal circles.[152]

A comparison of Lewis' Christology, and particularly his understanding of the nature of the incarnation and the atonement with, for example, Kenneth Cauthen's representatives of American evangelical liberalism[153] supports Craig's observation.

With regards to the incarnation, the starting point of all these theologians, as for Lewis, is not the supernatural Christ, but the human Jesus. Christ for them is to be regarded first and foremost as a human being. As John Lawton observes, "It became the watchword of all liberal Christology -- Christ's real humanity."[154]

Moreover, if Christ is to be understood in this

29

way, his personality must be available for study and observation as is that of every other historic person. This means that his being and his person must constitute a psychological unity. "No dogmatic fiction of one who appeared to act now with one personality -- the divine -- and now with another -- the human -- could ever serve as the basis for genuine critical study."[155] Thus liberal Christology found the traditional doctrine of the two natures of Christ untenable because it made Christ essentially different from the rest of humanity and presented a person who was inaccessible to historical research.

Related to this emphasis on Christ's real humanity is the other cornerstone of liberal Christology: the doctrine of divine immanence or the principle of continuity between human nature and God. This meant, as William Adams Brown puts it, "There is nothing in God's nature which separates him from any child of man."[156] It also provided another reason for dispensing with the traditional doctrine of the two natures. Since there was no longer any radical difference between humanity and divinity, such a doctrine simply was not necessary. In the words of Dillenberger and Welch, for liberalism, "the perfection of humanity _is_ the fullest embodiment of deity. The divine and human in Christ are not alien to each other abut are one."[157]

Based on these two assumptions, then, liberal theologians conceived of the divinity of Christ not in terms of incarnation, i.e. God becoming man, the divine invading the human from the outside; but in terms of immanence, i.e. God's presence within humanity, the perfecting of the divine in the human. Harry Emerson Fosdick's statement makes this clear:

> Divinity is not something supernatural that ever and again invades the natural order in a crashing miracle. Divinity is not some remote heaven, seated on a throne. Divinity is love. Here and now it shines through the highest spiritual experiences we know. Wherever goodness, beauty, truth, love are -- there is the divine. And the divinity of Jesus is the divinity of his spiritual life.[158]

Walter Rauschenbush uses different language than Fosdick but says essentially the same thing. Under the

influence of Schleiermacher and Ritschl he locates
Christ's divinity in the perfection of his spiritual
life, i.e. his unique God-consciousness.[159] Jesus is
"a perfect religious personality, a spiritual life
completely filled by the realization of a God who is
love."[160] Thus in basing the significance of Jesus
Christ on his moral excellence[161] and his divinity on
his absolute God-consciousness,[162] Lewis is not
original or unique, but is merely working within
standard liberal categories.

The same holds true in relation to his doctrine of
the atonement. Such doctrines are usually classified
as either objective or subjective. Those that are
objective maintain that redemption is contingent upon a
change outside of humanity such as in God or in the
situation in which humanity exists; those that are
subjective argue that such external changes are
unnecessary, and see redemption as contingent upon an
internal change in the attitude and orientation of
humans. Although these two types of these theories are
not mutually exclusive, theologians lean toward one or
the other. Liberals, in general, emphasize the
subjective aspect and thus see Christ's death in terms
of how it affects humanity.

Albert Knudson,[163] for example, argues that the
obstacle to salvation does not lie in God; He is always
loving and ready to forgive. The obstacle, rather,
lies in the selfishness, waywardness, and moral
indifference of humans. The death of Christ, then,
should be understood in terms of how it overcomes this
obstacle within men and women. It does this primarily
because of its revelational impact upon them:

> The presence of God in Christ gives
> immediate revelational value to his death,
> and the sacrificial love of God thus revealed
> awakens an answering love in the hearts of
> men. This is the only way in which sinful
> men can be redeemed, namely, through moral
> and spiritual transformation. No other kind
> of redemption would be truly Christian.[164]

Atonement, then, for Knudson, has little objective
bearing on God but is addressed to "the human need of
being morally empowered in order to overcome the drag
of nature on a free and virtuous but weak spirit."[165]

Essentially the same subjective or moral influence

theory of the atonement is found in Lewis' early Christology. Ransom, substitutionary, and governmental theories -- all which are predominately objective -- are frankly surrendered without apology. The death of Christ is necessary because repentance is the condition for forgiveness, and something must be done which, by revealing the nature of sin as it relates both to God and to humanity, will induce an adequate repentance in men and women.

Thus the Christology found in <u>Jesus Christ and the Human Quest</u> is a standard liberal treatment of the subject. In terms of its substance there is nothing novel or unique about it.

The Apologetic Form of Lewis' Christology

What is, however, unique to Lewis is the form or the shape in which his Christology is cast. Liberal Christology was, as has been suggested above,[166] anthropocentric in nature. It began "not with God and what he had done, but with man, and what man felt."[167] Moreover there were those who in determining the essence of humanity had argued, as Lewis did, that humans are fundamentally end-seeking creatures.[168] But no other theologian, in constructing his Christology, builds upon this assumption as Edwin Lewis does. The human quest is the basis of his entire formulation; his Christology flows out of it and returns to it again and again.

This brings us back to Lewis' underlying apologetic concern. By presenting the person and work of Christ in relation to the human quest he is trying to persuade the skeptic by showing that Jesus Christ meets and matches the need of humanity. Thus who he was and what he did is in keeping with the nature of things. He is not someone forced down upon us from above, but he fulfills and completes what we were meant to be. It is this apologetic form -- not its content -- which makes Lewis' Christology unique.

By presenting it in this manner Lewis is following the method of Olin A. Curtis,[169] his former teacher. In his systematic theology, Curtis breaks the traditional order of treatment and begins not with the doctrine of God but the doctrine of humanity. This involves an extended discussion of human personality in all of its various aspects. Later Curtis states that the purpose of following this order was "to secure an

32

anthropological foundation for Christian theology by showing that man's personal and moral development can be normally completed only under the terms of the Christian religion."[170] In constructing his Christology in the same manner Lewis has the same purpose in mind.

There is however, a difference between Curtis and Lewis, if not a difference in kind, then at least a difference in degree. An observation by Michael Ryan concerning Curtis' theology reveals this:

> What Curtis attempted to do, was not to derive his view of the Christian faith from his world-view, but rather to illuminate, to inform, and where necessary to correct his world-view from the standpoint of the Christian faith.[171]

Curtis, then, began with a world-view, but with a world-view already shaped and adjusted by the Christian faith. Lewis, on the other hand, began (as he himself recognized later on) with a world-view or philosophy "arrived at in the first place with no least reference to Christianity itself."[172]

In the case of Curtis, the result was a theology different in form, but essentially the same in substance as that of historic Christianity; with Lewis, however, though he sought to remain true to the historic faith, the difference extended to both. In form and substance his early Christology varied from the main lines of historic Christianity.

The Conservative Reaction to Lewis' Christology

Because it appeared at a time when the fundamentalist-modernist controversy was agitating the Methodist Episcopal Church,[173] Jesus Christ and the Human Quest came under the careful scrutiny of the conservative forces within the church, and especially their leader, Harold Paul Sloan.

Sloan and Lewis had been classmates at Drew Theological Seminary, and had studied together under Olin A. Curtis.[174] When "The Problem of the Person of Christ" appeared in the Methodist Review in January, 1923, Sloan had criticized it severely.[175] Although he claimed he had no hand in preparing them,[176] Sloan had

33

also been present at the Philadelphia Preachers' Meeting on February 12 when resolutions condemning the article had been approved.

On April 30, however, Lewis himself addressed the Preachers' Meeting[177] on the subject of divine redemption, and seemed to convince everyone there that his position was true to the historic faith. Following that meeting Sloan wrote to Lewis stating that he was in agreement with the view of the redemptive work of Christ which Lewis had presented, but felt it was incompatible with the conception of the person of Christ presented in his Methodist Review article:

After my conversation with you Monday I am re-established in my opinion of your position and it seems to me that the article in the Methodist Review is a very poor expression of your thinking. . . . I am persuaded that your effort in the Review was influenced by the naturalistic thinking which surrounds you in Northern New Jersey and New York City. It seems to me that it utterly fails to express you -- that it is a mediating view of no lasting significance. . . . If interpreted from the liberalistic point of view, so as to satisfy a thinker like Fosdick, your position becomes Unitarian. Jesus Christ becomes a human being powerfully influenced by the Divine and no more and the foundation of redemption is lost.[178]

Unconvinced that his theory of Christ's person was an inadequate basis for his theory of redemption, Lewis soon responded to Sloan's letter, stating the points at which the two agreed and differed, but maintaining that both of their positions were valid:

Respecting the fact that Christ is at once God and Man, you and I agree. Respecting the method and process involved we appear at present to differ. You believe that an eternal Divine self-consciousness entered into complete self-oblivion in the womb of Mary. I believe that an eternal Divine Consciousness at last absolutely identified itself with a Human Consciousness so that each became as the other. The result is the same . . . There is miracle in either case, and I think "my" miracle (if I may say

34

that) is just as wonderful . . . just as certainly a Divine self-sacrifice, as "your" miracle.[179]

In his reply to Sloan, Lewis also revealed how much he had been hurt by the Philadelphia Preachers' "resolutions."

> . . . do you not see where your Preachers' Meeting "Resolutions" have put me? They announced to the whole church that I had - in effect - surrendered the evangelical faith, and that I was unfit for my present position. They in substance labeled me as "heretic" as "Radical."[180]

Sloan wrote back expressing regret for the damage that had been done to Lewis by the "Resolutions." Nevertheless he justified the action of the preachers, and he also continued raising questions concerning the position Lewis had taken in his article:

> I have re-read your article in the light of your letters and of our conversation, and I cannot see but that its apparent meaning is even more divergent than your actual position. I do not see that you anywhere affirm that one of the three eternal Centres of self-consciousness of the Holy Trinity ever became identified with the man Jesus.[181]

As Sloan continued he became more and more hostile and defensive:

> You say you are wounded. I think we have occasion to feel wounded because of your article. I think we have occasion to feel wounded to a peculiar degree in your article above all others: for you are not hostile to historic Christianity as are Little and Peritz and many more within our Methodism....
>
> We fully appreciate that there is a working understanding on in Methodism for the suppression of the Historic Faith and for the promotion of rationalistic views. We know that bald infidelity is being taught in Methodist institutions. We chafe at the suppression of facts that is the policy of

our journals and at the spirit of arrogant intolerance with which all who oppose the rationalistic trend are treated.[182]

Because he was busy with pre-commencement activities, Lewis did not immediately respond to Sloan. Then on May 14 the Philadelphia Preachers' Meeting issued a statement condemning a report in the Christian Advocate which implied that because the preachers had approved of Lewis' address to them on April 30, their differences had therefore been settled.

When Lewis found out about their action he was deeply perplexed and dismayed. He expressed his frustration in his next letter to Sloan:

> It seems to me that, if I am correctly informed as to what took place and as to what was said, any further attempt on my part to elucidate my position is wasted effort. I confess that I am utterly unable to understand either the spirit or the motive of men who gave me such an enthusiastic vote on April 30, and then on May 14 condemned the Christian Advocate's very brief report of their own action, and of what it appeared to imply.[183]

Sloan admitted that he had been responsible for the action taken by the preachers.[184] The article in the Christian Advocate had been misleading, he maintained, because it implied that the preachers had withdrawn their former criticism and had endorsed Lewis' whole Christology when in fact they had only endorsed his view of redemption.

Later Neal D. Kelly, a close friend of Lewis' wrote to Sloan[185] wondering why, if he had had questions concerning Lewis' Christology, he had not brought them up at the April 30th meeting while Lewis himself was present instead of attacking his views later when he was not there to defend himself. Sloan replied to Kelley that he had brought up the issue of Christology on April 30, but that Lewis had side-stepped it. The fact that he accused Lewis of side-stepping the issue angered Kelley, and he wrote back demanding that Sloan retract his statement. Sloan refused, but in his response to Kelly's demand he did provide Kelly with further details concerning what had happened at the April 30th meeting:

36

I said: "Professor Lewis' position in Soteriology requires the Athanasian Christology. I wish he had expressed his views upon this subject also." Professor Lewis replied with a single sentence: "I accept the Athanasian Christology." It will be perfectly evident to every one that his Review article was in my mind when I raised this question, and it must have been evident to Professor also. That he replied by a single sentence was very disappointing to me, and I told him so afterwords. I later wrote to him to the same effect. It seemed to me, at the time, that he did intend to side-step the discussion of the questions raised by his article, nor can I now see how any other opinion is possible . . .[186]

When, however, Kelly told Lewis what Sloan had said, somehow the truth got twisted. According to the version of the story Lewis was told, Sloan had not only accused him of side-stepping the issue of Christology, but had implied that Lewis had "acted deceitfully" and "played a coward's part."[187]

Incensed, Lewis wrote to Sloan denying what he considered to be an unfounded accusation, and stating that "he resented it with every atom of feeling and strength he possessed."[188] He then wrote to the Philadelphia Preachers' Meeting and accused Sloan of duplicity and underhandedness in the whole matter.[189]

Thus even before Jesus Christ and the Human Quest was published Lewis and Sloan had been at odds with each other. Theologically they had differed sharply over their conceptions of the person of Christ, and unfortunately, those differences had eventually led to personal attacks upon each other.

Sloan's attacks upon Jesus Christ and the Human Quest, however, did not begin to appear until a year after the book had been released. In the interim he and a group of conservative pastors and laypersons had been busy organizing the Methodist League for Faith and Life. Founded February 3, 1925, at St. Paul's Church, Wilmington, Delaware, the purpose of the League was to repel the Modernist drive that was threatening Methodism as the Unitarian drive had threatened Congregationalism a century before.[190] The official publication of the League was The Call to Colors which

37

later merged with The Bible Champion to become The Essentialist. Sloan, who was president of the League, was its chief spokesman.

His first attack upon the Christology Lewis had set forth in his book did not, however, appear in the League's publication, but in the September 1925 issue of the Methodist Review.[191] Earlier Harris Franklin Rall had written a positive review of the book,[192] now Sloan was given the opportunity of presenting a dissenting opinion. In his review he criticized Lewis' view of the virgin birth, his conception of sin and punishment, his treatment of the universality of Christ, and his doctrine of the atonement, but his first objection -- "Professor Lewis has no real Incarnation"[193] -- was his major one. According to Lewis, Sloan argued,

> Jesus is not an eternal divine personality, the Second Person of the glorious Trinity, who took human nature and flesh in the womb of the Virgin; instead he is a man as we are who achieved progressively, and at death completely, a divine consciousness . . .

> For Professor Lewis Christ is divine only in the sense that with God's help he achieved a perfect expression of God's innermost motive and thought. He is eternal only in the sense that truth about God which came to expression in him is eternal . . .

> . . . Professor Lewis repudiates in its entirety that which the Christian Church has unanimously believed and maintained, namely, that the eternal personal Son of God took human nature and flesh in the womb of the Virgin; that personal God became man.[194]

This was the objection which Sloan repeatedly raised against Lewis' Christology during the next five years. Since he considered Jesus Christ and the Human Quest to be "the best discussion of the person of Christ from the modernist point of view"[195] he attacked it again and again particularly through the publications of the Methodist League for Faith and Life. As William Lewis points out in his study of the League,

> Beginning with the May, 1926, issue of the Call and continuing relentlessly through the

May, 1930 issue of the _Essentialist_, the
League periodical directed a steady barrage
at Edwin Lewis and Drew Theological Seminary.
No less than twenty articles were directed at
the teachings of Lewis during this period.[196]

Typical of those articles are statements such as
these:

Dr. Lewis of Drew reduces the Incarnation to
a DIVINELY INSPIRED HUMAN LIFE.[197]

Professor Lewis has sacrificed the
Theanthropic Person of the Creeds and offered
to faith once more a little Unitarian
Christ.[198]

Professor Lewis, like Unitarians and Arians
generally, still uses superlative language
about Jesus. But like other Unitarians he
has no idea that corresponds to the emotion
his words express.[199]

Professor Lewis' theory is not inductive, it
is not Scriptural, it is not loyal to the
historic Christian deposit. It is mediating
and arbitrary as all mediating views are.[200]

Thus the conservative attack upon Lewis was
relentless and unyielding. Although their request was
denied, at one point the League even asked the Board of
Bishops to investigate Lewis on the grounds that he was
teaching erroneous doctrine.[201] William Lewis is
correct, then, in his assessment that Edwin Lewis, more
than any other Methodist theologian bore the brunt of
the fundamentalist attack.[202] The controversy between
Lewis and Sloan was "the most notable and
representative confrontation of liberal and
conservative elements in the Methodist Episcopal
Church."[203]

The Controversy and Lewis'
Theological Transition

In the light of the change that was soon to occur
in Lewis' thinking, one cannot help but wonder what
part, if any, the controversy played in it. In his own
description of the factors that led to his change in
thinking he does not mention it. However, in reference
to _Jesus Christ and the Human Quest_ and its critics he

makes this interesting statement:

> The critics of the book directed themselves, naturally enough, to its theology. What they apparently did not see was that the theology was an attempt to ground Christianity in the type of philosophy just described [personal idealism].[204]

In thus assessing their attack Lewis was correct. His conservative critics did not seem to understand what he was trying to do. If they had they might have applauded his effort. He had set out to ground Christianity in a philosophy "arrived at in the first place with no least reference to Christianity itself."[205] The conservatives, however, did not understand that, or at least did not appreciate it. Instead they could only see areas where they felt the essentials of the faith had been abandoned.

This was undoubtedly frustrating to Lewis. He was trying to preserve the historic faith yet they were accusing him of destroying it. At the same time, however, their accusations and attacks did play a part (at least indirectly) in forcing Lewis to deal with a very essential question: Can you graft the Christian faith onto a philosophy arrived at apart from Christianity without in the process sacrificing the faith itself? Later Lewis came to the conclusion that it could not be done.[206] By forcing him, then, to deal with this question and thus to re-examine one of his basic presuppositions, the controversy did play a part in his theological transition. It is to an examination of that transition that we now turn.

1. David W. Soper, _Major Voices in American Theology_ (Philadelphia: Westminster Press, 1953), p. 21.

2. Edwin Lewis, _A Manual of Christian Beliefs_ (New York: Charles Scribners' Sons, 1927), p. 3.

3. _Jesus Christ and the Human Quest: Suggestions Toward a Philosophy of the Person and Work of Christ_ (New York: Abingdon Press, 1924), pp. 8-9.

4. "Annual Report to the Board of Trustees, Drew Theological Seminary, May 12, 1923," The Edwin Lewis Collection, Drew University, Madison, N.J.

5. Kenneth Cauthen, _The Impact of American Religious Liberalism_ (New York: Harper and Brothers, 1961), p. 5.

6. Ibid.

7. Harry Emerson Fosdick, _The Living of These Days_, p. vii, quoted in Cauthen, ibid., p. 27.

8. All the major Methodist theologians were, however, using Cauthen's distinction, "evangelical" rather than "modernistic" liberals. See Cauthen, ibid., pp. 26-30. See also William J. McCutcheon, "The Theology of the Methodist Episcopal Church During the Inter-War Period," Ph.D. dissertation, Yale University, 1960.

9. The only "non-liberal" was John A. Faulkner, Lewis' colleague at Drew. (See his _Modernism and the Christian Faith_ (New York: The Methodist Book Concern, 1921)). See also William J. McCutcheon, "American Methodist Thought and Theology, 1919-1960," p. 65.

10. Ibid., p. 21.

11. "Theological Expression and Contemporary Thought," _Methodist Review_ 105 (January 1922): 28.

12. Lewis had dealt with this at length in his

dissertation, "The Relation of Erasmus to Luther and Lutheranism as Revealed in Their Perspective Correspondance, and in the Writings of the Free-Will Controversy," Th.D. dissertation, Drew University, Madison, N.J., 1917. See also his article, "Erasmus and Luther: Their Relations During the Early Years of the Reformation," Methodist Review 99 (November 1917): 899-916.

13. "Theological Expression and Contemporary Thought," p. 29.

14. "From Philosophy to Revelation," p. 762.

15. "The Divine Triunity," Methodist Review 51 (March 1918): 275-293.

16. Ibid., p. 277.   17. Ibid., p. 278.

18. Ibid., p. 282.

19. See especially Personalism (Boston: Houghton, Mifflin and Company, 1908) and Theism (New York: American Book Company, 1902.

20. For a summary of Pringle-Pattison's thought see G. Watts Cunningham, The Idealistic Argument in Recent British and American Philosophy (Freeport, N.Y.: Books for Libraries Press, 1967), pp. 149-168.

21. There appears to be some confusion in Lewis' own mind as to when he read the book. In "From Philosophy to Revelation," written in 1939, he states, "In 1921 I read Pringle-Pattison's The Idea of God in the Light of Recent Philosophy" (p. 762). But in "The Divine Triunity," written in 1918, he says, "In understanding man we shall therefore come better to understand God. The method is justifiable, and has received fresh sanction in Pringle-Pattison's last book, The Idea of God" (p. 282). Thus Lewis was at least well acquainted with the book in 1918.

22. "From Philosophy to Revelation," p. 762.

23. Andrew Seth Pringle-Pattison, The Idea of God in the Light of Recent Philosophy (New York: Oxford University Press, 1920), p. 91.

24. Ibid., p. 103.   25. Ibid., p. 209.

26. Peter A. Bertocci, <u>The Empirical Argument for God in Late British Thought</u> (Cambridge: Harvard University Press, 1938), p. 52.

27. <u>The Idea of God</u>, p. 111.

28. Ibid., p. 112.   29. Ibid.

30. Ibid., p. 127.   31. Ibid.

32. Ibid., p. vii.   33. Ibid., p. 128.

34. Ibid., p. 153.   35. Ibid., p. 156.

36. Ibid., p. 252.   37. Ibid., p. 246.

38. Thomas A. Langford, <u>In Search of Foundations: English Theology, 1900-1920</u> (Nashville: Abingdon Press, 1969), pp. 67-70.

39. <u>The Idea of God</u>, p. 292.

40. Ibid., p. 315.   41. Ibid., p. 302.

42. Ibid., p. 304.

43. <u>Gott und Welt</u>, pp. 531-532, quoted in ibid., p. 305.

44. Lewis, "From Philosophy to Revelation," p. 762.

45. <u>The Idea of God</u>, p. 111.

46. Ibid., p. 157.

47. "The Problem of the Person of Christ," <u>Methodist Review</u> 106 (January 1923): 116-127.

48. Ibid., p. 117.   49. Ibid., p. 120.

50. Ibid., p. 124.   51. Ibid., p. 123.

52. Ibid., p. 125.   53. Ibid.

54. Ibid.

55. Letter, Edwin Lewis to R. B. Wells, 17 February 1923, Methodist Archives, Drew University, The

Harold Paul Sloan Papers.   Hereafter these will be referred to as HPS.

56. Ibid.

57. Letter, Thompson W. McKinney to Edwin Lewis, 10 March 1923, HPS.

58. Letter, Thompson W. McKinney to Ezra Squire Tipple, 8 February 1923, HPS.

59. Harold Paul Sloan, "Professor Lewis' 'The Person of Christ'," Eastern Methodist (March 1923):   3.

60. Ibid.

61. John A. Faulkner, "A Prominent Divine on Christ," Methodist Review 106 (March 1923): 292-296.

62. William B. Lewis, ibid., pp. 155-156. The information concerning the events surrounding the publication of the book is based on an interview with Edwin Lewis, March 5, 1957.

63. See A Manual of Christian Beliefs, pp. 66-98; and Great Christian Teachings (New York: Methodist Book Concern, 1933), pp. 47-63.

64. Lewis was a regular writer for the Adult Bible Class Monthly beginning in 1925. Much of what he wrote there was related to Christology, but see especially the following: "The Uncertainties and the Certainties of Jesus," (January-June 1930):   39; "The Final Proof of Jesus' Authority," ibid., p. 74; "Jesus' Loyalty," ibid., p. 213; "God's Need of Human Instruments," 24 (January-June 1931): 34; "Accounting for Jesus," 25 (January-March 1932):   33.

65. Jesus Christ and the Human Quest, p. 8.

66. Ibid., p. 7. See also p. 43, 85, 112, 219, 320, and 354 for statements indicating Lewis' commitment to personalism.

67. Ibid., p. 96.   68. Ibid., p. 18.

69. Ibid., p. 19.   70. Ibid., p. 21.

44

71. Ibid., p. 23.

72. Ibid., p. 34.

73. Ibid., pp. 30-33.

74. Ibid., p. 29.

75. Ibid., p. 48.

76. Ibid., p. 63.

77. Ibid., p. 87.

78. Ibid., p. 89.

79. Ibid.

80. Ibid., p. 90.

81. Ibid., p. 96.

82. Ibid.

83. Ibid.

84. Ibid., p. 99.

85. Ibid., p. 100.

86. Ibid., p. 97.

87. Ibid., pp. 98-99.

88. Ibid., p. 112.

89. Ibid., p. 113.

90. Ibid., p. 123.

91. Ibid., p. 126.

92. Ibid.

93. Ibid., p. 143ff.

94. Lewis has in mind the way redemption is presented in the ransom, penal substitution, and moral government theories of the atonement. Cf. note on pp. 151-152.

95. Ibid., p. 144.

96. Ibid., pp. 171-172.

97. Ibid., p. 173.

98. Ibid., p. 174.

99. Ibid.

100. Ibid., p. 177.

101. Ibid.

102. Ibid., p. 178.

103. Ibid.

104. Ibid., pp. 178-179.

105. Ibid., p. 180.

106. Ibid., p. 181.

107. Ibid., p. 191.

108. Ibid., p. 190.

109. Ibid., p. 192.

110. Ibid., p. 194.

111. Ibid., p. 195.

112. Ibid., p. 196.

113. Ibid., p. 197.

114. Ibid.

115. Ibid., p. 202.

116. Ibid., p. 204.

117. Ibid., p. 205.

118. Ibid., p. 213.

119. Ibid., pp. 218-219.

120. Ibid., p. 225.

121. Ibid., p. 235.

122. Ibid., p. 240.

123. Ibid., p. 242.

124. Ibid., p. 247.

125. Ibid., p. 250.

126. Ibid., pp. 250-251.

127. Ibid., pp. 256-257.

128. Ibid., p. 257.

129. Ibid.

130. Ibid., pp. 259-260.

131. This is the Greek word which is found in Philippians 2:5-11, the locus classicus of the kenotic theory.

132. Ibid., p. 273.

133. Ibid.

134. Ibid., p. 276.

135. Ibid., p. 277.

136. Ibid., p. 279.

137. Ibid., p. 284.

138. Ibid., p. 283.

139. Ibid., p. 291.

140. Ibid., p. 294.

141. Ibid., p. 295.

142. Ibid.

143. Ibid., p. 296.

144. Ibid., p. 297.

145. See pp. 11-13.

146. Ibid., p. 305.

147. Ibid., p. 306.

148. Ibid., p. 310.

149. Ibid.

150. Ibid., p. 307.

151. Ibid., p. 308.

152. S. G. Craig, Princeton Theological Review 23 (October 1925): 687.

153. William Adams Brown, Harry Emerson Fosdick, Walter Rauschenbush, Albert Knudson, and Eugene Lyman. See Cauthen, ibid., pp. 41-143.

154. John S. Lawton, Conflict in Christology: A Study of British and American Christology, from 1889-1914 (London: Society for Promoting

Christian Knowledge, 1947), p. 8.

155. Ibid.

156. Modern Theology and the Preaching of the Gospel,
p. 104, quoted in Lloyd J. Averill, American
Theology in the Liberal Tradition (Philadelphia:
Westminster Press, 1967), p. 72.

157. Protestant Christianity, p. 219, quoted in
Cauthen, ibid., p. 80.

158. The Hope of the World, p. 103, quoted in ibid.,
p. 80.

159. Ibid., pp. 104-105.

160. A Theology for the Social Gospel, pp. 154-155,
quoted in ibid., p. 105.

161. See above, pp. 14-16.   162. See above, p. 27.

163. See the discussion of Knudson's view in Robert
E. Chiles, Theological Transition in American
Methodism: 1790-1935 (Nashville: Abingdon
Press, 1965), pp. 175-180.

164. Basic Issues in Christian Thought, p. 148,
quoted in Robert Chiles, ibid., p. 177.

165. Cauthen, ibid., p. 125.

166. See above, pp. 29-30.

167. Lawton, ibid., pp. 13-14.

168. Jesus Christ and the Human Quest, p. 40.

169. See Olin A. Curtis, The Christian Faith:
Personally Given in a System of Doctrine (New
York: Eaton and Mains, 1905), pp. 7-112.

170. Ibid., p. 183.

171. Michael D. Ryan, "The Theology of Olin Curtis,"
Drew Gateway 41 (Winter 1971): 83.

172. Lewis, "From Philosophy to Revelation," ibid.,
p. 762.

173. For an account of the fundamentalist-modernist controversy within Methodism, see McCutcheon, "American Methodist Thought and Theology, 1919-1960," pp. 267-273. Methodism, however, as McCutcheon points out, was the least affected of all the major denominations by the controversy.

174. Apparently the two men even had their disagreements then! See Harold Paul Sloan, "The Review of 'Jesus Christ and the Human Quest,'" The Essentialist 3 (November 1927): 167.

175. See above, pp. 10-11.

176. Letter, Harold Paul Sloan to Edwin Lewis, 8 May 1923, HPS.

177. The address was subsequently published. See "Human Nature and the Christian Redemption," Methodist Review 107 (January 1924): 35-47.

178. Letter, Harold Paul Sloan to Edwin Lewis, 3 May 1923, HPS.

179. Letter, Edwin Lewis to Harold Paul Sloan, 5 May 1923, HPS.

180. Ibid.

181. Letter, Harold Paul Sloan to Edwin Lewis, 8 May 1923, HPS.

182. Ibid.

183. Letter, Edwin Lewis to Harold Paul Sloan, 16 May 1923, HPS.

184. Letter, Harold Paul Sloan to Edwin Lewis, 17 May 1923, HPS.

185. Harold Paul Sloan to the Methodist Preachers' Meeting of Philadelphia and Vicinity, 17 February 1924, p. 1.

186. Ibid., p. 4.   187. Ibid., p. 1.

188. Ibid.   189. Ibid., pp. 1-2.

190. McCutcheon, ibid., p. 271.

191. Harold Paul Sloan, "Jesus Christ and the Human Quest -- A Criticism," Methodist Review 108 (September 1925): 800-807.

192. Harris Franklin Rall, Review of Jesus Christ and the Human Quest by Edwin Lewis, in Methodist Review 107 (November 1924): 966-969.

193. Sloan, "Jesus Christ and the Human Quest -- A Criticism," ibid., p. 801.

194. Ibid., pp. 801-802.

195. Harold Paul Sloan, The Christ of the Ages (New York: Doubleday, Doran and Co., 1928), p. 122.

196. William Lewis, ibid., p. 161.

197. "The Next Major Battlefield in Methodism: Professor Lewis of Drew Theological Seminary Denies the Deity of Christ," The Essentialist 3 (December 1927): 194.

198. Ibid.

199. "Professor Edwin Lewis of Drew University Teaching Unitarian Views," The Essentialist 6 (May 1930): 42.

200. "'Essentialist's' Case in the Debate on the Person of Christ," The Essentialist 6 (May 1930): 42.

201. "The Board of Bishops are Informed," The Essentialist 3 (November 1927): 166.

202. William Lewis, ibid., p. 165.

203. Ibid., p. 153.

204. Lewis, "From Philosophy to Revelation," p. 762.

205. Ibid.   206. Ibid.

Chapter 2

FROM PHILOSOPHY TO REVELATION

The Spread of Naturalistic Thinking

Lewis first began to question his early theological position as he witnessed the rapid spread of naturalistic thinking -- "especially evolutionary naturalism and the closely related naturalistic theism"[1] -- in liberal theological circles. As an evangelical liberal his primary concern in expounding a theology within the philosophical framework of personal idealism had been to "preserve the great evangelical emphases of Christianity."[2] In achieving that end he used philosophy because he believed it made the faith more credible to the modern mind. But always, his chief concern was to establish the validity of the Christian revelation. Philosophy, for Lewis, was merely a means toward accomplishing that end; it never was an end in itself.

However there arose within liberalism during the mid-1920's, a movement which made revelation secondary and subservient to philosophy. Led by Douglas Clyde Macintosh, Henry Nelson Wieman, Shailer Matthews, and Edgar Sheffield Brightman,[3] the philosophical "realists" were in revolt against the idealism of earlier liberalism and were determined to undermine it. Classified by Cauthen as "modernistic" liberals, in contrast to the "evangelical" liberals[4] they insisted that all truth be judged by the standards of modern empirical science, including the truths of the Christian revelation. If, accordingly, a truth was judged unacceptable, it was either to be modified or abandoned. Thus for the modernistic liberals,

> The standard by which the abiding values of Christianity of the past were to be measured was derived from the presuppositions of modern science, philosophy, psychology and social thought. Nothing was to be believed simply because it was to be found in the Bible or Christian tradition.[5]

That such a movement did eventually arise to challenge evangelical liberalism was inevitable. Sooner or later all mediating positions tend to move away from center in one direction or another. Evangelical liberalism, in attempting to mediate between faith and reason proved to be no exception. As H. Richard Niebuhr later pointed out in his critique of liberalism,

> No mediating theology in history has ever been able to keep in balance the opposing elements it seeks to reconcile, and this truth held for the American mediators also. As time went on liberalism began to outweigh Evangelicalism more and more. At the same time the former tended to become increasingly secular . . . . In the course of succeeding generations the heritage of faith with which liberalism had started was used up.[6]

But though the leftward shift in liberalism may have been inevitable, it nevertheless caused Edwin Lewis great concern. "I saw that a purely rationalistic approach to the problem of existence, and much more to the problem of religion could very easily yield conclusions utterly destructive of all I took the Christian faith to be."[7] It also forced him to question the validity of what had been his primary concern up to that time, i.e., the grounding of the Christian faith in philosophy.[8] For although the conclusions the modernistic liberals arrived at were radically different from his, their methodological approach to theology was essentially the same. Both began with a philosophy "arrived at in the first place with no least reference to Christianity itself."[9] Their conclusions were different than his because they began with a different philosophy, but since they adhered to the same basic methodology were their conclusions any less legitimate?

Walter Marshall Horton, who went through a theological transition similar to Lewis', accurately depicts the dilemma in which evangelical liberals, confronted by the rising tide of naturalism in their ranks, found themselves:

> But when the humanists appeared on the scene with their Gospel of salvation by scientific research and cooperative effort, the dilemma of liberalism became acute. The humanists professed to be the real moderns, and it must be admitted that their position

represented, in some respects a logically consequent outworking of principles to which the liberals themselves had appealed . . . If now they refused to carry out these principles to the bitter end, what reason could they give for their refusal?[10]

As Lewis struggled with this problem, he eventually came to believe that his basic approach to theology had to change. Although it was an honest attempt, he came to the conclusion that what he had been trying to do -- graft theology onto philosophy -- could never be done:

> . . . it became increasingly clear to me that Christianity could not be "adjusted" to any kind of a priori philosophy, because it contains its own philosophy, and the elements in it which give rise to this are such as no purely a priori philosophy could either discover or accept.[11]

Lewis' Discovery of the Bible

Yet at the same time that Lewis was having growing doubts about his earlier approach to theology, there was also a growing certainty in his mind as to what the Christian faith essentially called for:

> It called, I became convinced, for a living God, a God who knows that he is God, who knows what he is doing and why he is doing it; a God who is prior to his creation, and other than his creation, and who in his creation is fulfilling a purpose which he himself freely chose; a God who is related to men, not by the operation of some ontological necessity, but by his own free creative act; a God to whom sin is a reality and an offense, and something that he cannot away with; a God so constituted that he was able to enter into his creation by a specific act of incarnation, so profoundly concerned for sinful men that he would do this, and yet withal so fundamentally different not only from his creation but also from man himself (the truth in totaliter aliter, "the wholly other") that the act of incarnation and all that goes with it must involve an unimaginable disruption of his very being,

must therefore be for him tragic and
sacrificial, costly to the uttermost point of
which he was capable. "God, who spared not
his own Son . . ."[12]

This growing certainty was prompted by what Lewis
himself described as "my discovery of the Bible."[13]

In 1926, Lewis was asked to be co-editor with F.C.
Eiselen of a one-volume Bible commentary to be called
The Abingdon Bible Commentary.[14] Feeling unqualified
for the task since his expertise was in theology and
not biblical studies, Lewis accepted the offer "most
unwillingly and only under very strong pressure."[15]

When it was finally published three years later,
more than sixty scholars from around the world had
contributed to the commentary. Lewis himself was
responsible for two of the major articles;[16] but the
real significance of the project lay in his great
editorial labors. Due to his many other obligations
and his failing health, Eiselen was unable to keep up
with the demands of the project. As a result the
publishers rearranged the work load making Lewis
responsible for much the greater share. This included
the proof-reading, verifying all the scripture
references, and supplying almost all the cross-
references. As he went through the commentary for the
fifth time, Lewis prepared an index which was 42
double-column pages in length. This constant exposure
to the scriptures had a profound influence on his
thinking. As he describes it,

For the three years during which the
Commentary was in process, I was under
necessity of living with the Bible daily.
Whether I would or not, it was my meat and
drink, and the experience revolutionized my
thinking. I saw with devastating clarity
that speculative philosophy whether it got as
far as supernaturalism or whether it stopped
with naturalism, could never accomodate
itself to Christianity. Instead, it required
Christianity to do the accomodating, and that
was something that could not be, if
Christianity as represented in the New
Testament, and as climaxing what was given in
the Old Testament was to be taken seriously.

I found myself faced with the Word of

God, given it is true, by slow processes
through the words of men, but at last in
Christ, "made flesh." The Creator appeared
as the Redeemer. He who acted in the primal
miracle of creation acted again in the
miracle of redemption. I saw that this must
be either true or not true. It if be not
true, then have we nothing but the confusions
of naturalism. But if it be true -- and it
must be true if we are to have enduring hope
-- it can be true only as something revealed,
not as something discovered. Creation and
the incarnation are alike acts of God, and
each has its meaning, but we know the act and
we know the meaning because, and only
because, they have been _disclosed_ to us.[17]

Lewis had thus moved "from philosophy to
revelation," and his "discovery of the Bible" was
undoubtedly the major reason for the shift in his
thinking. He had seen "with devastating clarity" the
utter futility of all attempts to accomodate the
Christian revelation to fit the demands of philosophy
-- a process that could not be carried out without
mutilating the revelation at its most essential points.
The central doctrines of Christianity "could be held
true only on the ground that they had been
'revealed'."[18] Furthermore, revelation could stand on
its own. It did not need to be adjusted to an outside
philosophy in order to be credible; it contained its
own philosophy within itself.

God and Ourselves

That a change was taking place in Lewis' thinking
could first be detected in _God and Ourselves_ published
in 1931. Written in response to the spread of
naturalistic thinking described above,[19] the book was
an apologetic for theism, or as Lewis termed it, the
God of "the Great Tradition." In the face of those who
wanted to redefine God as Value, Process, or something
else, and those who like E.S. Brightman, wanted to
limit God,[20] Lewis sought to present "a frank and
unabashed statement of the faith of our fathers
concerning a God who is real, a God who is adequate, a
God who is available."[21]

Against those who assert that God can never be
more than a rational working hypothesis, he begins his
apologetic by arguing for "the right to be certain."

Since intellectual effort based on philosophical and scientific reasoning alone cannot yield religious certainty, the issue, Lewis maintains, ultimately hinges on the place given to religious experience: "Is there a type of experience of which the correlative is that reality we call God?"[22] For Lewis the answer to that critical question is a definite Yes, and he bases his case for religious certainty upon that Yes:

> That there may be a God can be shown by reasons that would be called good respecting any other fact: we therefore get our "probability." That there is a God is the testimony of religious experience, the experience being held to require a correlative in reality just as much as any other type of normal experience: we therefore get our "certainty."[23]

Having thus established his case for the reality of God on the validity of religious experience Lewis proceeds to argue for divine adequacy. Taking issue with the prevalent denial of naturalism with regard to the sovereignty of God, he maintains that views which postulate a "growing" God or a "finite" God or a God in some sense impotent, "are not a sign of intellectual daring, as is so often assumed, but of intellectual hesitancy."[24] Granted that there are perplexing problems growing out of a belief in divine sovereignty, such a belief "answers to every feature of life no less adequately than non-theistic naturalism, and in addition explains those higher reaches of existence and of experience as naturalism never can."[25]

Next Lewis poses the question concerning the sovereign goodness of God. In the face of suffering, natural evil, and death there have been those who have felt it necessary to deny God altogether, or to present God as "finite," "growing," "struggling," or in some way "limited."[26] Lewis, however, points out the shortcomings of these positions and defends the conception of God found in traditional theism. He argues that those who, in the face of evil, deny God altogether, are still left without a solution to the problem of evil. They also cannot adequately account for the presence of good in the world. Those who would limit God in order to relieve him of responsibility for the perplexities of life end up "vesting with uncertainty the whole outcome of the cosmic travail."[27] On the other hand, traditional theism, contrary to what some think, does not close its eyes to the perplexities of life. But in the face of these, still holds to a "belief in a God who makes provision for those very inevitabilities that seem to deny him, or at least to circumscribe or harass him, but who is at the same time a God whose will, seen in its total reach and purpose, these inevitabilities express and carry out."[28]

The same can be said about "the moral shadow," i.e., the fact of sin. Considered apart from the overall purpose of God sin "becomes an insoluble problem in the universe of such a God as we believe God to be."[29] But seen in the light of the good which God ultimately desires for humanity, it is apparent that the possibility of sin is a necessary condition for the attainment of that good. Does this however, mean that God wants sin?

No; God does not "want" sin. What he "wants" is virtue, moral goodness, holiness. Only, he can have this only by having sin as well. And he would rather have sin as an inevitable concomitant of the process whereby he seeks and obtains goodness than not have the goodness because he would not have the sin.[30]

The possibility of sin, however, involves a great cost to God himself. "The moral shadow that lies across the world falls on him as the shadow of a cross."[31]

God, then, is not only the world's Creator; He is also its Savior -- a fact which for Lewis implies three things. First, God serves. As the part must serve the whole, so the whole must serve the part. The entire tree serves its smallest leaves and branches, just as these parts make the tree as a whole what it is. This principle also applies to God: "If nothing could be but for God, then God is the servant of all that is . . . . his universal lordship and his universal service are inseparable."[32]

Second, God suffers. Because of the nature of reality, his service is a suffering service. To affirm this does create certain metaphysical problems, but there is no better or reasonable alternative. "Without the idea of a suffering God there is no way of moralizing the cosmic movement conceived as the steady expression of a benevolant creative Will."[33] The world's travail is therefore also his travail. We may

57

not be able to adequately explain what transpires within his being when God undergoes the experience of suffering, but this does not lessen our insistence on the fact that he does suffer. "A holy God cannot be implicated in the process of evil without suffering."[34]

Finally, God saves. Out of his travail comes new life. "The Universal Servant who is the Universal Sufferer becomes thereby also the Universal Savior."[35] In the light of this, what shall we say?

> We shall say that God can justify his method. We shall say that the disvalues that necessarily go with the method cannot discount the values: the joy of the gain and the sadness of the loss are parts of the same organic whole -- and the whole is worth while.[36]

This, then, is the case for theism which Lewis presents in God and Ourselves. We have summarized it in order to suggest the contrast between this volume and his earlier work, Jesus Christ and the Human Quest. Whereas earlier he had argued for the rights of the modern mind and was constantly calling into question the traditional understanding of the Christian faith; now he is on the other side doing just the opposite. Again and again he defends "the God of the great tradition" in the face of the modernist attack.

Lewis' case for theism, however, only makes up the first half of God and Ourselves, and in the second half he presents the case for the idealistic philosophy underlying his view. Since that philosophy has already been outlined,[37] it will not be discussed here. The fact, however, that Lewis finds it necessary to present an extended argument for idealism also sheds light on his theological transition. Later he claimed that God and Ourselves was "the first definite expression"[38] of his new position. Although he conceded that because it was primarily a critique of the various contemporary naturalisms, "it said little about the specific Christian revelation,"[39] he still insisted,

> . . . it ought to be clear to anyone who reads the book that it is the Christian God who is presented, especially in the claim that God is the Universal Servant who is the Universal Sufferer and becomes thereby also the Universal Savior. This is no rational

deduction. Rather it is one of Tertullian's amazing "incredulities."[40]

Yet in spite of what Lewis maintained, it is evident that in <u>God and Ourselves</u>, although there has been some shift in his thinking, the transition "from philosophy to revelation" was not yet complete but was still in process. That this is the case can be seen clearly in Lewis' discussion of the nature of revelation itself. Throughout his discussion he stresses that revelation is a cooperative endeavor involving not only divine initiative but human discovery as well. As he explains it,

> The inner and the outer "worked together" to do what neither could do alone . . . . All that we mean by civilization, and eventually by the kingdom of God, is but the exhibition of this cooperative principle on an everwidening scale.

> There is still no better way of describing this process than by the word "revelation."[41]

McCutcheon, therefore, rightly concludes: "In this book Lewis brought under criticism all such naturalisms but did not emerge as a champion of the exclusiveness of Christian revelation initiating solely from God and finding a response of faith in men."[42]

In 1931 then, Lewis had not completely moved away from his earlier position. He was still enamored with idealistic philosophy, and had not yet fully come to see as he would later on that "Pringle-Pattison with his steady insistence on universal continuity could make no proper place for what A.E. Taylor calls 'the initiative of the Eternal,' or W.E. Hocking 'the divine aggression.'"[43]

In his assessment of <u>God and Ourselves</u>, David Soper notes, "the argument struggles stubbornly in the Nessus shirt of an apologetic spirit. It is a polemic, not a song."[44] The "song," of course, would come later; but perhaps it was for this reason that the book had little impact,[45] and the change which was taking place in Lewis went largely unnoticed.

Re-Thinking Missions

In 1933, however, Lewis wrote two articles which left little doubt in anyone's mind that a change had occurred. The first of these,[46] which appeared in the April issue of the Drew Gateway, was Lewis' critical review of Re-Thinking Missions, a volume containing the report of the Commission of Appraisal of the Layman's Foreigh Mission Inquiry.

Concerned that growing doubts among the laity over the validity of the missionary enterprise was causing declining contributions for missions work, this Inquiry had been established in 1930 to observe and evaluate missionary work in Asia. The thirty-five directors of the Inquiry were drawn from seven denominations[47] and its Commission of Appraisal included William E. Hocking who served as chairman, as well as Arlo Ares Brown, president of Drew. Although the various mission boards cooperated with the project it was carried out independently so that its findings might be more objective.

The Inquiry was conducted in two stages. First, in the fall of 1930, a corps of fact-finders from the Institute of Social and Religious Research was dispatched to India, Burma, China, and Japan. After spending almost twelve months investigating and then formulating their observations, they returned with what Kenneth Scott Latourette described as "the most careful, objective study of a large cross-section of Protestant missions ever made."[48]

Then the second stage of the project began. The fact-finders turned their materials over to a Commission on Appraisal. With those materials in hand, the members of the Commission then visited the four countries themselves, observed missionary work, and interviewed various Christian and non-Christian leaders. Finally, after numerous lengthy sessions, they drafted the final report.

Because the work of the Inquiry had been widely publicized, the report was awaited with great anticipation. Each week, as its various parts were released to the public, the editorial section of The Christian Century furnished its readers with summaries of their content.[49] Finally, the complete report was made public on November 18, 1932 and published under the title Re-Thinking Missions. Immediately it became a storm center of controversy, bursting "like a thunderclap on a great portion of the American church."[50]

The majority of the report dealt with the practical aspects of the missionary enterprise such as the Church, education, Christian literature, medical work, agricultural missions, missions and its role in industry, and women's interests and activities. There was also a section on the administrative aspects of missions. Yet it was not the criticisms and recommendations for change in the majority of the report which sparked the most controversy; rather it was the first section of the report which called for a revised understanding of the relationship between Christianity and other religions, and a revised conception of the finality of Christ.

With the rise of materialism, secularism, and naturalism, the Commissioners argued, a new situation has arisen which "compels a thorough reanalysis of the purpose of missions in reference to other faiths."[51] Traditionally the non-Christian religions had been looked upon as enemies of Christianity, the one true religion. Now, however, in the face of a new enemy, the secular spirit, that approach must be altered. Thus it is necessary that modern missions "make a positive effort, first of all to know and understand the religions around it, then to recognize and associate itself with whatever kindred elements there are in them."[52]

In turn, Christian missionaries should not look upon themselves as bearers of a definite message to those who practice other religions, but as "brothers in a common quest."[53] Of paramount importance is that quest itself; the route need not be prescribed. The furtherance of the quest "may be by way of the immediate strengthening of several of the present religions of Asia, Christian and non-Christian together."[54] Often the quest has been encrusted with superstition and tainted with selfishness, but it has continued nonetheless, sustained and driven on by that "germ," that "nucleus," which is the basis of all the creeds: "the inalienable religious intuition of the human soul."[55]

It is the God of that intuition who is the true God; and it is that God who Jesus, through his inherently simple teachings, sought to reveal. Because "the insistent problems of religion came to Jesus with peculiar clarity and force," his teachings "may be taken as final."[56] Since his whole life was given over to "manifesting the meaning of religion," it stands "as a unique support to all who subsequently desire to carry out the same venture."[57]

Yet although Christianity affirms the uniqueness of the religion practiced by Jesus, it does not have the right to make absolutist or exclusivist claims. It is still one among many religions, and though it has much to give, it also must be willing to receive. It has a right to spread its teachings, but it can learn from the teachings of other religions too. Understood in these terms, the aim of Christian missions can thus be defined: "To seek with people of other lands a true knowledge and love of God, expressing in life and word what we have learned through Jesus Christ, and endeavoring to give effect to his spirit in the life of the world."[58]

This, then, was the "re-thought theology" of the Laymen's Commission which created such a furor across the American church.[59] In fact discussion was so intense that for the next six months The Christian Century contained editorials and articles related to the report.[60] The majority of these, though by no means uncritical, reflected the liberal bias of the journal and were in basic agreement with the conclusions of the Inquiry. There was, however, a strong negative reaction to the report among conservatives within the denominations. Typical of these was the lengthy article written by Presbyterian missions secretary, Robert Speer, which was soon issued as a pamphlet and circulated among the churches.[61]

Thus in a provocative editorial, "Is Modernism Ready?," The Christian Century tried to assess the situation. The Laymen's Report, it stated, reflects "the changed status of modernism in the churches."[62] In the past liberals, for the sake of unity, had accepted "the ecclesiastical status quo." Now, however, that had changed:

But that period of silent and uncritical acquiescence has passed, and the Laymen's report is the signal that it has passed. Since the transition of Protestantism from the traditions of old-school theology began in the late years of the nineteenth century, this is the first time that modernism has acted explicitly, and upon its own initiative, to effect the reconstruction of any primary function of the Christian church. It can mean only one thing, namely, that modern ideals have so permeated the thought of the church's effective leadership that the uncritical acquiescence in the established routine of church life is no longer morally possible.

. . . The Laymen's Report signalizes distinctly the obsolescence of dogmatic orthodoxy and the emergence of an effective and responsible modernism.[63]

The editorial, however, also stated that this advance of modernism would not go unchecked by the forces of orthodoxy. The result, then, could be a conflict as acute as the fundamentalist-modernist controversy of a decade before. So it concluded,

A major battle looms on the horizon of Protestant Christianity. It is no academic battle of ideas, this time, though it will bring to play the whole ideology of both traditional and modern thought. But the basic functioning of organized Christianity is involved.[64]

Thus when Edwin Lewis' article appeared in the <u>Drew Gateway</u>, the battle lines over the Laymen's Report had already been drawn up; and based on his earlier writings, it would have been natural to assume that he would take his stand alongside those who favored the report. But to almost everyone's surprise, he took the opposite position.

At the beginning of the article Lewis expressed profound gratitude for the Commissioner's report: "They have said, in a way that practically guarantees a church-wide hearing and consideration, things that lesser voices have been saying for years without much apparent effect."[65] He then listed many of the assertions in the report with which he agreed.

What followed, however, was a severe attack on the Commissioner's understanding of the essence of Christianity. They have presented one view, said Lewis, "But it still remains that <u>another</u> view is

63

possible -- a view that would make room for practically everything positive that the report contains, but would contain certain vital elements that the Report omits."[66] He then spelled out what those vital elements were:

> The Commissioners have aimed in all sincerity to reach down into the inwardness of Christianity and bring to light its "substance." They are against a doctrine-centered message . . . But, after all, the claim that in Jesus Christ God did something that he had never done anywhere else, and that what he did unites with an aggressive divine grace on the one hand and the tragedy of human sin on the other, and that Jesus Christ was not simply a supremely religious man and the first Christian but rather a fresh and original manifestation of the Creative Will, so that yesterday, today, and forever, he is the Lord of Christians because he is the means of their deepest experience, and that it is through him alone that God purposes -- and has eternally purposed -- to reconcile all men to himself, meaning to achieve the complete divine-human unity -- this claim is not merely a matter of formal literary expression, but it is of the very substance or essence of Christianity.[67]

Unfortunately this conviction -- "the bedrock in all Christian expansion"[68] -- was missing from the Report. Consequently, the ultimate goal of Christian missions -- to bring all persons under the Lordship of Jesus Christ -- had been compromised for "a sort of polydaemonistic Parthenon in which Jesus Christ will be but one of many."[69]

Lewis concluded his article by expressing surprise and disappointment in Professor Hocking. For many years he had held Hocking in the highest regard and had personally benefitted from his writings.[70] But he could not reconcile Re-Thinking Missions with Hocking's earlier writings, particularly his chapter on "The Divine Aggression" in Human Nature and Its Re-Making. There Hocking had argued that human experience itself necessitates a God who takes the initiative in revealing himself. "God must intervene. God must break into the circle in which we are caught."[71] Moreover, what human experience calls for is exactly what the Christian faith maintains has been provided. God is thus

> . . . one who invades the earth in order to bring men to themselves . . . He disguises himself, takes the form of a servant . . . is despised and rejected and done to death . . . He appears in the temporal order . . . He suffers, not alone with us (as any god must who knows what is going on), but also for us and at our hands . . . It is such a god, active in history and suffering there, that Christianity declares as the most important fact about the world we live in.[72]

Lewis therefore wondered if he had mistaken the logic of such statements by Hocking; and if not, why was that logic so absent in the re-thought theology of the Report?

Later he admitted that writing the article had not been easy. Nevertheless, because he was convinced that what the Report presented was "a virtual abandonment of the Christian gospel as presented in the New Testament and historically understood,"[73] he felt compelled to go ahead. "The threads that were still binding me to my former compromises were broken not without some 'sadness of farewell' -- and I went a way I could no longer evade."[74]

In response to his article Lewis received a number of letters, some expressing gratitude for the position he had taken, and others disdain. Hazen Warner, who was later elected bishop, thanked him for helping to put courage in the hearts of many pastors who were "feeling the impact of these present-day disillusionments."[75] On the other hand, Jesse Lacklen, a District Superintendent, was disappointed in what he perceived to be the "new Lewis." He wondered how such a leader in the church could be "in company with Sloan and Machen even on one issue."[76]

The Fatal Apostasy

Then in the fall of 1933, Lewis' article, "The Fatal Apostasy of the Modern Church,"[77] appeared in Religion in Life. In this hard-hitting emotionally charged essay, he blamed theological liberalism for the plight of the modern church:

We yielded positions whose strategic significance is becoming more and more manifest. We so stressed the Bible as coming to us in "the words of men" that the sense in which it is also "the word of God" has become increasingly vague. We so freely allowed the influence of contemporary forces in the development of doctrine as to have endangered the continuity of that living core of truth and reality for which contemporary forces were but the <u>milieu</u> . . . And in particular we were so determined to recover for the church "the human Jesus" that we lost sight of the fact that the church is the creation of "the divine Christ" or at least of faith in Christ as divine. Have we sown the wind, and is the whirlwind now upon us?[78]

Liberalism with its emphasis on "the religion of Jesus" attempted to redefine the supernatural elements in the New Testament doctrine of Christ to bring them in line with modern thinking. Those elements, it maintained, were later accretions and thus part of the substance of the gospel. What it forgot was that "the Gospels are themselves the product of a community which already had "seated Christ at the right hand of God," and that, "failing that audacious act of their mind and heart, we had no gospels at all."[79]

Lewis went on to graphically describe the fruits liberalism had borne in the churches:

How far have we gotten with our various substitutes? Look over our churches: they are full of people, who brought up on these substitutes, are strangers to those deeper experiences without which there had been no New Testament and no Church of Christ. Thousands of clergymen will go into their pulpits next Sunday morning, but not as prophets . . . Those who come to listen will not be brought face to face with eternal verities. Hungry sheep will look up, but will not be fed.[80]

In order to be "saved" Lewis urged the churches to "re-enthrone Christ," not simply as a man who had lived and died but as

a Contemporary Reality, a God whose awful

holiness is "covered" by one who is both our representative and his, so that it is "our flesh that we see the Godhead," that "flesh" which was historically Jesus of Nazareth but is eternally the divine Christ whose disclosure and appreciation Jesus lived and died to make possible.[81]

Lewis concluded his article with an impassioned plea to the churches to return to their historic beliefs. "O Church of Christ everywhere, on the avenue, down the side street, in the town square, at the cross-roads would that thou believedst as thou should!"[82]

Because of its explosive nature, the article attracted wide attention particularly within American Methodism. Lewis received a host of letters. Most of them expressed gratitude for the position he had taken. Bishop Ralph Cushman called it "a great prophetic message," and added, "I don't believe you can realize how much it means to our confused preachers to hear a man in your position witness in this day."[83] Bishops Leonard, Lowe, and even Welch in far-away China also commended Lewis. But perhaps the most moving letter came from S.H. Shutleff, a pastor in Madison, South Dakota. Shutleff lamented the many Methodist pastors, who because of their liberal theology, had no gospel to preach: "They worship at the sign of the question mark, think any enthusiasm bad form, and the only word in their religious vocabulary is adventure." Then he praised Lewis for what he had done: "My, oh me! But you really did tell 'em. And how! Your article in the current number of Religion in Life is the most straight from the shoulder utterance along lines of religious thought that I have read for many a day. And you really dared to use the word -- 'apostasy'."[84]

There were, however, a number of letters which were extremely hostile. Lewis was accused of having "gone Barthian," having "sold out to the Fundamentalists," having become "senile and conservative," and so on.[85] Thus partly to answer his critics, and partly to elaborate his new position, that winter Lewis expanded his article into what was to become his most celebrated book, A Christian Manifesto.

The Influence of Barth

Before, however, discussing that book and its

67

impact, it will shed light on Lewis' theological transition if we examine one of the charges mentioned above that was leveled against Lewis, namely that he had "gone Barthian."

Early in 1933, prior to the publication of the two articles we have been discussing, The Christian Century published two articles[86] by Lewis on the theology of Karl Barth. The first of these was an address Lewis had given at Drew in the fall of the previous year. Printed in booklet form it somehow found its way to The Christian Century where, without Lewis' prior knowledge, it was reprinted in the January 18 and 25 issues.

Throughout the article Lewis applauded Barth and urged the American church to hear what he was saying. He recounted Barth's disillusionment with theological liberalism, the influence of Kierkegaard and Dostoievsky, Luther and Calvin, Barth's Commentary on Romans, his repudiation of Schleiermacher, and his acceptance of the primacy of revelation. Then he discussed the main lines of the new theology: its eschatological dimension, its emphasis on the word of God, divine transcendence, and its "crisis" orientation. Finally, Lewis summed up the impact of Barth's theology:

> That it is a revolutionary message is undeniable. It is a direct assault upon so-called modernism. It cuts the ground from under the feet of many of our so-called "programs." It says "goodbye" to the concept of evolution as applied to the relations of God and man. It strikes a terrific blow at our human pride and boasted self-sufficiency. It is a message designed to send us to our knees in deep penitence . . . A preacher who can read Barth without being driven to his knees in a deep heart searching must have become so inexpressibly callous that he could remain unmoved even if Christ himself should suddenly meet him in the way.[87]

From the content and tenor of the article, many were left with the impression that Lewis had become a follower of Barth. Two months later, however, The Christian Century published Lewis' article "Where is Barth Wrong?" which had been written at the request of the editor. Here he outlined the major deficiencies of

68

Barth's theology. First of all, Lewis felt that Barth made the wrong use of a right principle by carrying the infinite qualitative distinction between time and eternity to an extreme. As a result Barth could not allow for God's presence in anything temporal. But, asks Lewis,

> How can you say "God is not here," unless already "God" has some meaning for you? Or how can you say, "God is here; he lays hold upon me; he has found me," unless in some measure you already possessed the God who finds you? We can grant all that Barth says about the divine initiative -- no deeply religious man would deny it -- but the initiative is toward one who is inherently approachable and who is able to respond.[88]

For Lewis the basis of all religion is the kinship between God and humanity, a kinship which proves that the infinite qualitative distinction between the divine and the human is not absolute. In the experience of reconciliation the "metaphysical antagonism" between the two gives way to a "moral triumph." "What cannot logically be, actually is. The far God is the near God. God seeks, but he is also sought, and the being sought is but the human side of the divine seeking."[89]

Secondly, Lewis faulted Barth for his authoritarianism. In his effort to guard against religious subjectivism, Barth maintained that revelation comes through the men of the Bible, and nowhere else. Thus he would have us believe in God solely on the basis of their testimony, and would exclude any experience of God we ourselves might have. Against this extreme objectivity, Lewis argues that a second-hand knowledge of God is really no knowledge at all. "If the transcendent God is not _here_, how do I know that he was ever _there_? If he does not speak to _me_, I can too easily question that he speaks to _you_."[90]

Lewis leveled his third major criticism at Barth's Christology. For Barth the Jesus of history has given way completely to the Christ of eternity. His docetic Christology is the result of his metaphysic of absolute divine-human antithesis, and is "one of the most glaring examples of a _priorism_ that the history of theology can show."[91]

Based on Lewis' critique it is clear that he was

never merely an echo of Barth, nor was the charge that he had "gone Barthian"[92] justifiable. Though he was in agreement with Barth in his insistence on the fact and necessity of divine revelation, he could never go along with his absolute "Nein" to natural revelation, or "his virtual rejection of philosophy as a proper ally of theological thought."[93] Lewis therefore always insisted that Barth's influence on him had been indirect. In terms of its actual content his theology was closer to Emil Brunner's than to Barth's.

He did, however, credit Barth with giving him something very important: courage. In light of the prevailing theological climate, his shift "from philosophy to revelation" which was being precipitated by his "discovery of the Bible" was not easy. Reading Barth helped in giving him the courage to see it through. As Lewis himself explained:

What therefore Barth chiefly did for me -- and it was a great deal -- was to help me find the courage, at an important period in my life to throw off the shackles of mere contemporaneity and keep my mind "exposed" to the Bible in the effort to determine the nature and the significance of the Christian faith.[94]

Thus in analyzing the change which took place in Lewis' thinking, Charley Hardwick is correct in maintaining that it "should be characterized as analogous to rather than derived from Barth's change because just as with Barth, it was not the reading of another theologian but the study of the original sources themselves that occasioned the reorientation."[95] Yet though Barth's influence was indirect, it was significant nonetheless. He helped to give Lewis the courage and determination to stay with the sources.

The Manifesto

A Christian Manifesto, published in 1934, "marked the climax in the defining of the new position."[96] A manifesto, by definition, is a public declaration of one's principles or intentions. Lewis thus sought to make explicit "the meaning of what had 'happened,'"[97] to him. Addressed to the American churches at large, the book burns with extreme urgency and passionate intensity. The result is, as McCutcheon describes it, "a broadside proclamation rather than a systematic and reasoned apologia."[98]

Lewis begins by chastising the modern church for its "needless retreat" from the historic faith. Convinced that it had to choose between the historic faith and modern thought, the modern church chose the latter. It thus tried to adjust its beliefs to modern categories, or was silent about them while stressing its ethical and social features. This attempt, however, was futile, for it overlooked something essential:

> . . . when the Christian ethic is divorced from the Christian faith, it becomes the world's supreme example of the fatal antithesis of a splendid idealism and the necessary power of attainment. What more pathetic than a noble eagle whose wings have been clipped: great aspirations, but earthbound feet![99]

The attempt was also based on a false assumption, for the historic faith and the modern mind are not essentially incompatible. Modernity may make the ancient questions more insistent, but it does not invalidate the answers the historic faith has given. Thus there is no need to retreat. "We have a faith. Let us be done with forever half-heartedly apologizing for it, and instead let us aggressively, confidently, and self-forgetfully proclaim it."[100] The essence of that faith, the "trunk-line" running down the Christian centuries, is a belief in Jesus Christ as "One in whom God lived and acted as he lived and acted in no one else, and who thereby became the suffering Savior of men."[101]

It is also that belief which lies at the heart of the New Testament. Granted there are difficulties which confront us when we approach the New Testament. In it we find human documents, which are culturally conditioned and which present diverse viewpoints. In dealing with them we should thus feel free to use every resource of critical scholarship. However, the difficulties in the New Testament need not present a stumbling block to faith,

> . . . provided always that we see in the New Testament not the historical basis of the faith, but, rather, <u>the</u> <u>witness</u> <u>to</u> <u>that</u> <u>basis</u>, which is a quite different thing. Any:

71

damage that has been done by criticism has resulted from the fact that already a false view of the New Testament was being entertained. Men stopped with the book whereas they should have gone beyond the book to that which made the book possible.[102]

According to Lewis what made the book possible was the resurrection of Jesus Christ. That event provided the basis for the faith to which they gave witness in the New Testament, and so ultimately everything hinges upon it. Some, of course, will object that by staking the Christian faith on the resurrection, Lewis is "trying to make an incredible faith credible by the help of something that is more incredible still."[103] Lewis, however, believes there is no alternative: "The Jesus of history passed for evermore into the Christ of faith by reason of the resurrection as actual fact. If that be denied, the New Testament falls apart, and the history of Christianity is the history of a vast delusion."[104]

The inescapable logic of this is that Christianity _means_ supernaturalism, and only a philosophy which makes room for the supernatural can adequately provide a framework for its faith. Failing to realize this, the modern church succumbed to the pressures of modern thought and sought to establish an alliance with naturalism. "The result was a compromise which, in the nature of the case could not be permanent. Christianity always loses when it compromises."[105]

Lewis again argues that such a compromise was unnecessary. In fact trends in the very science and philosophy which liberalism sought to please point in the direction of supernaturalism. As examples he cites the conception of the universe as multiverse, the growing conviction that existence cannot be reduced to a completely rational system, the inappropriateness of applying categories derived from one aspect of existence to another aspect of a totally different nature, and the validity of Plato's four-fold path to reality. All these "justify the same conclusion, namely, that the ineradicable supernaturalism of Christianity need be no barrier to the modern mind."[106]

Given this "ineradicable supernaturalism," it is possible to rehabilitate the claims of the historic Christian faith, and in what follows, this is what Lewis attempts to do. He affirms first of all, the reality of God and the authority of the Bible as the Word of God. The work of biblical criticism was needful and necessary, but unfortunately the resulting change in our understanding of the _form_ of the word "left us sadly confused as to the _substance_."[107] For Lewis, however, that substance is clear:

> The least we can say is that the Bible is the Word of God because unless God had spoken and men had heard, it would never have been written. It has its basis in a divine initiative, and is itself the evidence to a human response to that initiative. Indeed if you like to have it so, it is a human production, but the production is because of the inspiration of God. God spoke and men heard: this is what you cannot escape, explain it how you will and express it in what terms you will.[108]

Lewis further affirms that Christianity is "a religion of regeneration,"[109] because it maintains that human nature both can and needs to be changed. The necessity of regeneration is based on "the fact of sin both as status and deed."[110] This doctrine -- the Christian doctrine of human sinfulness -- has been subject to endless attacks in recent years; nevertheless, it is essential to the Christian faith and must be adhered to firmly. Thus Lewis asserts that

> . . . there is a fundamental disharmony at the very center of original human nature, that this is an inheritance which we do not ourselves choose, and that specific sinful acts are its inevitable issue . . . the stubborn fact stands: sinful status is not merely the sum-total of so many separate and specific deeds, but it is already implied as a fact in the deeds themselves.[111]

In the two chapters which follow, "The Atoning Deed," and "The Incarnate God," Lewis moves on to discuss the divine solution to the situation created by human sin -- a solution which is rooted in the atonement and incarnation of Jesus Christ. Many considered these chapters the most illuminating and inspiring in the book, but since they exhibit Lewis' revelation-centered Christology which will be outlined in the following chapter, they will not be discussed here.

73

Then Lewis again addressed the churches of American Protestantism, and particularly his own Methodist Episcopal Church. In graphic terms he recounted what had happened over the past decades:

> Anyone who knows the life of our church for the last twenty years or so knows that under the goading of the "experts" we have adopted scheme after scheme, participated in drive after drive . . . We have created in the minds of many a totally false conception of the nature and the function of the Christian Church . . . We borrowed our criteria of evaluation from the world about us -- a world gone mad in its worship of mere size . . .[112]

Again he emphasized the reason for the Church's current malaise: "Because as a church we listened too readily to those who assured us that unless we spoke a new language the world would not heed our message."[113] Thus above all else, the Church must recover the message of original Christianity. "It is to the proclamation of that message that the church is called to return -- and, let it be added, to an incarnation of the message in its own life and work."[114]

Because of its nature, Lewis' _Manifesto_ evoked immediate and intense reactions all across the church. Soon after its publication, letters concerning it began pouring in. The majority expressed appreciation for the book and for the courage it had taken to write it. A Methodist pastor from Woodbury, New Jersey, thanked Lewis for his "defense of the gospel."[115] Another from Alpena, Michigan wrote that the _Manifesto_ had "sounded THE note that must be sounded in trumpet tones."[116] William Seitter from Dawson, Pennsylvania, called it the "most significant production in the past fifty years."[117]

Letters commending the book were also received from Bishop Titus Lowe and Bishop Nolan B. Harmon, Jr. Philadelphia pastor, Clinton Cherry, noted, "Your style is at its best despite the white heat at which you write, and on the margin of one page at least I have noted: 'Like poetry.'"[118] Agreeing with Lewis' description of the modern church he declared:

> The church has lived on borrowed faith long enough. The loan has given out.

"Liberal" preachers with an emasculated gospel have presumed on the really faithful to the point of exhaustion. The secret is out -- and unless the church swings back to the essential supernatural gospel, its days are numbered.[119]

Even Harold Paul Sloan applauded Lewis, and rejoiced at his clear statement of the historic faith. Concerning his chapter, "The Incarnate God," he wrote, "Its majestic sentences thrilled me again and again."[120] He was also instrumental in getting the New Jersey Annual Conference and the Philadelphia Preachers' Meeting to pass resolutions commending the book.[121]

On the other hand, there were also letters extremely critical of the Manifesto. Norman Twiddy, a former student of Lewis', expressed dismay "that such a leader of constructive liberalism as you should be so dogmatically defending a neo-Calvinistic view of men and God."[122] He could not believe that the same person who had written the Manual and the Quest could also have written chapters 6-8 of the Manifesto.[123] He noted the bewilderment among other former students at what appeared to be "theological backtracking" on the part of their professor. "We fear," he concluded, "that your revolt against humanistic tendencies and against naturalism has swung you too far back to the 'abandoned dugouts.'"[124]

Ohio pastor John Versteeg also attacked Lewis. He quoted a recent comment by a Methodist bishop who in reference to Lewis had said, "Whenever a man gets ready to take a mental nosedive, he credits the Lord with the idea."[125] He further expressed alarm that such a church leader would speak "in terms of a Barthian automaton."[126]

It was these same Barthian tendencies in the Manifesto which upset Jonathan B. Hawk, an editor of Adult Sunday School publications in the Methodist Episcopal Church:

> If I had to admit that man's nature was essentially sinful, I could certainly not accept any redemption that might be offered. I could not bring myself to trust a Creator who had made me essentially wicked and then found it necessary to redeem me from that

wickedness before he could count me worthy of
his grace and to the ultimate life which we
Christians think he is going to give us."[127]

In addition to the many letters, the book was also
reviewed in many theological journals. Harris Franklin
Rall, who earlier had written a positive review of
Jesus Christ and the Human Quest, assessed the
Manifesto in the Christian Century. This time,
however, he expressed disappointment in Lewis.
Concerning several of the book's major emphases --
humanity's sinful status related to creatureliness and
not specific deeds; a sovereign God who had the right
to smash men and women if that is what He saw fit to
do; God's holiness necessary to his nature, but his
mercy optional; an incarnation based completely on a
one-way movement -- in all these Rall felt that Lewis
had fallen under the spell of Karl Barth. He agreed
that a new understanding of a living, personal,
transcendent God was badly needed, but concluded, "I
believe that the way out is forward, and not by
retracing our theological steps."[128]

Perhaps the most famous critique of the book was
Bishop Francis McConnell's which appeared in Religion
in Life.[129] After initially expressing gratitude for
the book's clear statements on the trustworthiness of
biblical revelation and the divinity of Christ,
McConnell noted what he felt were its major
deficiencies. First, the author was prone to over-
exact statements of truths which were better left implied than made explicit. For example, from his
emphasis on depravity and human sinfulness, one could
easily conclude that the road to hell is paved with the
skulls of infants. McConnell was certain that Lewis
never intended to say that, but because of his extreme
statements such an inference could be drawn.

McConnell also faulted Lewis for his extreme
statements with regard to divine sovereignty. Lewis'
God he observed, is "a fairly gritty Being," and at
times "can do quite a bit of smashing." In that our
preaching of the divine fatherhood had become "the
preaching of the divine grandfatherhood," it was time
someone emphasized God's sovereignty. But again, Lewis
overstates his case by emphasizing one aspect of truth
to the neglect of its balancing counterpart. He is
"much more eloquent when he is talking about smashing
than when he is talking about grace, that we remember
the smashing longer."[130] Finally, McConnell questioned

whether Lewis' charge of apostasy with regard to the recent programs of the church was legitimate. "All that section inveighing against the recent large-program activities of Methodism is oratory -- good oratory -- but oratory just the same."[131]

It was in response to Bishop McConnell's review that Harold Paul Sloan wrote to The Christian Advocate. In the past, he stated, he had always appreciated McConnell's insightful reviews and articles, but this time he was extremely disappointed:

> The bishop has totally missed the majesty and power of this book's burning message. Here is a book that is vibrant with the authentic voice of the Triune God calling the Church back to its essential mission; and Bishop McConnell, raising questions, almost irrelevant, seems to have missed the roll of its divine thunder.[132]

The editor of The Christian Advocate also responded more favorably to the Manifesto than McConnell had. He assured his readers that this was not "simply the record of a surrender, a Radical turned Tory,"[133] neither was it the sacrifice of the social aspects of Christianity for a purely personal gospel. In assessing its significance he noted:

> There have been other signs of a spiritual thaw in sunny nooks where the frost has lingered long. The ice-bound brooks are beginning to flow, the buds are swelling. That is the effect which this thrilling book has had upon at least one reader who has been impatient for the summer of faith to come again.[134]

Such were the many and varied responses to A Christian Manifesto. In looking back several years later, Lewis conceded that if he were rewriting the book there were some points he would modify, yet he was still convinced that the book "with all its faults of over-emphasis, represents the real meaning of the Christian revelation."[135] In contrast to the Quest which had been "an attempt to graft the gospel on a philosophy," the Manifesto was "an attempt to take the gospel 'as is,' to expound its amazing and overwhelming content . . ."[136]

77

From Liberalism to Neo-Orthodoxy

With the publication of <u>A Christian Manifesto</u>, Lewis' theological transition "from philosophy to revelation" was complete. This transition can be overemphasized, and so it is important to also stress that it was in no way a complete break with the past. S. Jameson Jones has this in mind when he states that "the theological biography of Edwin Lewis has more unity and coherence than is usually assumed."[137] In the same vein, Lynn Harold Hough, Lewis' colleague at Drew, maintained that just as there was "an implicit evangelical center in his earlier thought," so there was "an implicit liberalism in his forceful dialectic for classical Christianity."[138] There are, then, elements of continuity in all his theology.

It is also important, however, not to downplay his transition or fail to grasp its radical nature. In his perceptive study of the shift from liberalism to neo-orthodoxy in American theology,[139] Dennis Voskuil distinguishes between "chastened" liberals and "converted"[140] liberals, using the former term to describe those theologians who merely modified their former position, and reserving the latter for those who evidenced a radical reorientation in their thinking. He places Lewis in the "converted" category, and rightly so. The change which occurred in his thinking was dramatic and definite; for his uppermost concern at one time -- providing a philosophical basis for the Christian faith -- had been replaced by another -- expounding the revelation of God in Christ.

Mention of Voskuil's study and his distinction between types of theological transitions which occurred among liberals also leads us to another fact about Lewis' transition which needs to be stressed; namely, that although the change which took place in Lewis had certain unique features, it was similar to the change which took place in a number of liberals during the same time period. Voskuil thus includes Lewis with seven others -- Walter Marshall Horton, Reinhold Niebuhr, H. Richard Niebuhr, Wilhelm Pauck, Elmer G. Homrighausen, Walter Lowrie, and George W. Richards -- all former liberals who either changed or modified their positions during the early thirties, and who became the formulators of American neo-orthodoxy.[141]

There were a number of factors which contributed to the change occurring in these men. Several have

78

already been discussed in relation to Lewis' transition, but it will be helpful to review those factors as well as to mention others so that we can grasp how his transition was related to the transition which was taking place in American theology as a whole.

First of all, there were certain crisis events, such as World War I, the Great Depression, and the rise of totalitarian governments, which drained liberals of much of their earlier optimism about human nature. There is, of course, differing opinion concerning the extent to which these events influenced liberalism. Sydney Ahlstrom, for example, downplays the influence of the War. In the years following the War, he maintains, "Liberalism, like America in general, continued to speak in the old way as if nothing much had happened. Overhead the banner of Normalcy fluttered listlessly."[142] William Hutchinson, however, states that the effect of the war "ought not to be minimized." To support his contention, he quotes Reinhold Niebuhr's statement concerning the impact of the war on him: "When the war started I was a young man trying to be an optimist without falling into sentimentality. When it ended and the full tragedy of its fratricides had been revealed, I had become a realist trying to save myself from cynicism."[143]

Dennis Voskuil, on the other hand, while noting the influence of the War, argues that the Depression actually had a greater impact on liberalism: "If the war struck the initial blow for realism, the economic collapse during the early thirties delivered the coup de grace. More than any other crisis event, the Great Depression facilitated a shift away from moralistic liberalism."[144]

There is, then, disagreement over the extent to which these crisis events created a disturbance within liberalism, and disagreement over which event was most disturbing. But who would discount their influence altogether? Altogether they cast a long shadow upon the fundamental liberal belief in the goodness and improvability of human nature.

Along with these crisis events, the "crisis theology" of Karl Barth also had a provocative effect upon liberalism.[145] Americans were not really introduced to Barth's theology until March, 1926, when Gustav Krüger, professor of church histosry in Giessen, Germany, lectured on the "theology of crisis" at Union

Theological Seminary in New York. His lectures, published in the Harvard Theological Review, finally allowed Americans to read something in English about this theology which was creating such a stir in Europe.

Barth's first book to be translated into English was The Word of God and the Word of Man which appeared in 1928. Its translator, Douglas Horton, a young Congregation pastor in Brookline, Massachusetts who had studied in Germany before the War, happened to pick up this collection of Barth's essays while browsing through the new-book shelf at Harvard Divinity School. Three decades later Horton pondered the effect of that providential encounter:

> At first I glanced idly through it for the chapter titles then found myself reading some of the more arresting paragraphs, and presently succumbed so completely to the spell of its passionate intensity and penetrating faith that I lost track of the passage of time -- not to be brought back to myself for two or three hours . . . Only those who are old enough to remember the particular kind of desiccated humanism, almost empty of otherworldly content, which prevailed in many Protestant areas in the early decades of this century, can understand the surprise, the joy, the refreshment which would have been brought by the book to the ordinary and, like myself, somewhat desultory reader of the religious literature of that time.[146]

The Word of God and the Word of Man was widely read and reviewed.[147] It was followed by a number of interpretative articles on Barth. Then came book-length assessments of his theology such as Wilhelm Pauck's somewhat critical, Karl Barth: Prophet of a New Christianity, published in 1931, and Walter Lowrie's much more positive Our Concern With the Theology of Crisis which appeared the following year.

Thus little by little, the voice of Karl Barth began to be heard in America; and although there was considerable resistance to certain tenets of his theology, its impact -- more provocative than persuasive -- was being felt.

Another factor which contributed to the breakdown

of liberalism was the result of an intellectual collaboration between two very unlikely parties: the fundamentalists and secular humanists. As Hutchison points out in his discussion of the attack of this "odd couple" on liberalism, the very fact that two such widely divergent groups were able to agree "suggests how pervasively the flaws of the liberal posture were being felt."[148]

The point at which they agreed was in their contention that the choice between orthodoxy and liberalism was not a choice between two different interpretations of Christianity, but a choice between Christianity (orthodoxy) and no Christianity at all (liberalism). This was the argument of both J. Gresham Machen in Christianity and Liberalism (1923) and Walter Lippman in Preface to Morals (1929).[149] And although liberals such as Shailer Matthews and Harry Emerson Fosdick seemed to successfully counter it, the fact that the attack was coming from both sides -- the extreme right and the extreme left -- had an unsettling effect upon liberalism.

Thus as a result of these various external factors -- crisis events, Barthian theology, and the unified attack of fundamentalism and humanism -- there was a growing internal critique within liberalism during the late twenties and early thirties. Christian Century editor, Charles Morrison, conceded that liberalism was impotent,[150] Henry P. Van Dusen diagnosed its sickness,[151] and John Bennett even spoke of its demise.[152] The most devastating internal critic, however, was Reinhold Niebuhr.[153] In his various books and articles[154] he chided liberalism for its moral bankruptcy, its lack of ethical potency, and above all, its sentimental and naive optimism. In 1932, his Moral Man and Immoral Society appeared. According to Ahlstrom it was "probably the most disruptive religio-ethical bombshell of domestic construction to be dropped during the entire interwar period."[155]

The year, however, which marked the point of no return in the transition to neo-orthodoxy was not 1932, but 1934.[156] During that eventful year a number of volumes were published which reflected the change which had taken place in American theology. Come Holy Spirit, a collection of sermons by Barth and Thurneysen, translated and edited by George W. Richards and Elmer Homrighausen, appeared as did Richard's own Beyond Fundamentalism and Modernism, The Gospel of God.

So did Walter M. Horton's <u>Realistic Theology</u>, and perhaps most important, Reinhold Niebuhr's <u>Reflections on the End of an Era</u>.

The year 1934 also brings us back to Edwin Lewis, for it was in that year that his <u>Manifesto</u> appeared. Our brief account of the collapse of liberalism and the rise of neo-orthodoxy thus serves to underscore the fact that his transition, "from philosophy to revelation," was typical of a transition which was taking place in American theology as a whole. The factors which had caused him to rethink his earlier position were also having a telling effect in other liberal quarters; and the notes which he had begun to sound -- the primacy of revelation, the sovereignty of God, the depth of human sinfulness -- were being echoed by many others all across the land.

1. "From Philosophy to Revelation," p. 762.

2. Ibid.

3. See especially Macintosh, <u>Theology as an Empirical Science</u> (New York: The Macmillan Co., 1919); Wieman, <u>Religious Experience and Scientific Method</u> (New York: The Macmillan Co., 1924); Matthews, <u>The Faith of Modernism</u> (New York: The Macmillan Co., 1924); Brightman, <u>The Problem of God</u> (Nashville: Abingdon Press, 1930).

4. For this distinction between types of liberals see <u>The Impact of American Religious Liberalism</u>, pp. 29-30, and above, p. 8. For the limitations of classifying liberals according to this type, however, see William R. Hutchison, <u>The Modernist Impulse in American Protestantism</u> (Cambridge: Harvard University Press, 1976), pp. 7-8.

5. Cauthen, <u>The Impact of American Religious Liberalism</u>, p. 29.

6. H. Richard Niebuhr, <u>The Kingdom of God in America</u> (Hamden: The Shoe String Press, 1956), p. 194.

7. "From Philosophy to Revelation," p. 762.

8. See above, pp. 2-3.

9. "From Philosophy to Revelation," p. 762.

10. <u>Realistic Theology</u>, p. 3, quoted in William R. Hutchison, ed., <u>American Protestant Thought: The Liberal Era</u> (New York: Harper and Row, 1968), p. 192.

11. "From Philosophy to Revelation," p. 762.

12. Ibid., pp. 762-763.   13. Ibid., p. 763.

14. Frederick C. Eiselen, Edwin Lewis, and David G. Downey, eds., <u>The Abingdon Bible Commentary</u> (New York: The Abingdon Press, 1929).

15. "From Philosophy to Revelation," p. 763.

16. "The Miracles of the New Testament," pp. 921-939; and "The New Testament and Christian Doctrine," pp. 944-950.

17. "From Philosophy to Revelation," p. 763.

18. Ibid., p. 762.   19. See pp. 77-81.

20. God and Ourselves (New York: The Abingdon Press, 1931), p. 13. For Brightman's view see his The Problem of God, and The Finding of God (New York: The Abingdon Press, 1931).

21. God and Ourselves, p. 14.

22. Ibid., p. 24.   23. Ibid., p. 25.

24. Ibid., p. 55.   25. Ibid., p. 65.

26. Ibid., p. 74.   27. Ibid.

28. Ibid., pp. 83-84.   29. Ibid., p. 130.

30. Ibid., p. 131.   31. Ibid., p. 139.

32. Ibid., p. 140.   33. Ibid., p. 148.

34. Ibid., p. 159.   35. Ibid., p. 160.

36. Ibid., pp. 162-163.   37. See above, pp. 12-21.

38. "From Philosophy to Revelation," p. 763.

39. Ibid.   40. Ibid.

41. God and Ourselves, p. 234.

42. William J. McCutcheon, "American Methodist Thought and Theology, 1919-1960," p. 305.

43. "From Philosophy to Revelation," p. 762.

44. Major Voices in American Theology, p. 23.

45. According to Caldwell, the book was reviewed in only four journals, in contrast to Jesus Christ and the Human Quest which was reviewed in fifteen. See John Caldwell, Edwin Lewis: An Enumerative Bibliography, pp. 75-76.

46. "The Re-Thought Theology of 'Re-Thinking Missions,'" Drew Gateway 4 (April 1933): 3-6.

47. Baptist (Northern), Congregational, Methodist Episcopal, Presbyterian Church in U.S.A., Protestant Episcopal, Reformed Church in America, United Presbyterian. See Re-Thinking Missions (New York: Harper and Brothers, 1932), p. ix.

48. Kenneth Scott Latourette, "The Layman's Foreign Missions Inquiry: The Report of its Commission of Appraisal," The International Review of Missions 22 (April 1933): 155.

49. See "Should Foreign Missions be Continued?," The Christian Century 49 (October 12, 1932): 1228; "Actualities in the Mission Field," (October 19, 1932): 1259-1260; "Are Missionaries Competent?," (October 19, 1932): 1260; "The Outlook for Mission Schools," (October 26, 1932): 1293-1294; "Attacking the Laymen's Mission Inquiry," (November 2, 1932): 1323; "The Whole Church Under Review," (November 9, 1932): 1363-1364; "Not Doctrine but New Life is the Need," (November 9, 1932): 1364; "The Use of Foreign Money in Christian Missions," (November 16, 1932): 1396; "Is the Missionary Enterprise Spread too Thin?," (November 16, 1932): 1396-1397; "The Selection and Training of Missionaries," (November 23, 1932): 1429; "A New Order of Missionaries," (November 23, 1932): 1429-1430.

50. Paul Hutchinson, "The Laymen's Mission Report," The Christian Century 49 (December 21, 1932): 1577.

51. Re-Thinking Missions, p. 29.

52. Ibid., p. 33.   53. Ibid., p. 31.

54. Ibid., p. 44.   55. Ibid., p. 37.

56. Ibid., p. 55.   57. Ibid.

58. Ibid., p. 59.

59. For the wide range of responses see "Reaction to the Laymen's Report," The Missionary Review of the World 56 (January 1933): 43-45.

60. See Pearl S. Buck, "The Laymen's Mission Report," The Christian Century 49 (November 23, 1932): 1434-1437; "Is Modernism Ready?," (November 30, 1932): 1462-1464; "The Laymen's Mission Report Before the Boards," (December 14, 1932): 1532; Frederick B. Fisher, "Re-Thinking Missions," (December 14, 1932): 1538-1540; Paul Hutchinson, "The Laymen's Mission Report," (December 21, 1932): 1576-1578; Frank Rawlinson, "What Will the Laymen's Report Do to the Missions?," (December 28, 1932): 1604-1606; "Has the Laymen's Report Been Misunderstood?," The Christian Century 50 (January 4, 1933): 3-4; George E. Sololsky, "What Matters in Missions?," (January 11, 1933): 52-54; "Bringing the Laymen's Report to the Middle West," (January 25, 1933): 107; Charles E. Raven, "What is the Christian Message?," (February 1, 1933): 149-151; "Dr. Speer on the Laymen's Report," (February 8, 1933): 184-186; E. Stanley Jones, "China and the Laymen's Report," (February 15, 1933): 220-221; Frank Kingdon, "The Pagan Taint in Missions," (March 1, 1933): 285-287; H. Paul Douglas, "Missions at the Crossroads," (April 12, 1933): 491-492; "Kagawa and the Missions Report," (May 24, 1933): 680-681; Toyohiko Kagawa, "Missions Without the Cross," (May 24, 1933): 685-687; Raymond P. Carrier, "Re-Thinking Missions in the Colleges," (June 21, 1933): 813-815.

61. "An Appraisal of the Appraisal," The Missionary Review of the World 56 (Jaunary 1933): 7-27.

62. "Is Modernism Ready?," The Christian Century 50 (February 8, 1933): 185.

63. Ibid., pp. 1462-1463.   64. Ibid., p. 1464.

65. "The Re-Thought Theology of Re-Thinking Missions," p. 4.

66. Ibid., p. 5.   67. Ibid.

68. Ibid., p. 6.   69. Ibid., p. 5.

70. "From Philosophy to Revelation," p. 764.

71. "The Re-Thought Theology of Re-Thinking Missions," p. 6.

72. William E. Hocking, <u>Human Nature and Its Re-Making</u>, pp. 422-423, quoted in ibid.

73. "From Philosophy to Revelation," p. 764.

74. Ibid.

75. Letter, Hazen Warner to Edwin Lewis, 17 May 1933.

76. Letter, Jesse Lacklen to Edwin Lewis, 5 May 1933.

77. "The Fatal Apostasy of the Modern Church," <u>Religion in Life</u> 2 (Autumn 1933): 483-492.

78. Ibid., p. 483.   79. Ibid., p. 484.

80. Ibid., p. 488.   81. Ibid., p. 487.

82. Ibid., p. 492.

83. Letter, Ralph S. Cushman to Edwin Lewis, 18 October 1933, Drew University, The Edwin Lewis Collection. Hereafter these will be referred to as ELC.

84. Letter, S.H. Shutleff to Edwin Lewis, 23 October 1933, ELC.

85. Lewis, <u>A Christian Manifesto</u> (New York: The Abingdon Press, 1934), p. 9.

86. "What is Barth Trying to Say?," <u>The Christian Century</u> 50 (January 18, 1933): 120-121; "Where is Barth Wrong?," (March 22, 1933): 385-387.

87. "The Theology of Karl Barth," p. 121.

88. "Where is Barth Wrong?," p. 385.

89. Ibid.   90. Ibid., p. 386.

91. Ibid.

92. Hutchison observes that "Barthianism" became a "code word, even among the neo-orthodox, for an unacceptable transcendentism, anti-intellectualism, and ignoring of social responsibility." <u>The Modernist Impulse in American Protestantism</u>, p. 300. It was at these very points that Lewis too found Barth

unacceptable.

93. Lewis, "How Barth Has Influenced Me," _Theology Today_ 13 (October 1956): 358.

94. Ibid.

95. Charley Hardwick, "Edwin Lewis: Introductory and Critical Remarks," p. 95.

96. S. Jameson Jones, Jr., "Three Representative Leaders in Contemporary American Methodist Theology," p. 201.

97. _A Christian Manifesto_, p. 10.

98. William J. McCutcheon, "American Methodist Thought and Theology, 1919-1960," pp. 307-308.

99. _A Christian Manifesto_, p. 19.

100. Ibid., p. 28.   101. Ibid., p. 50.

102. Ibid., p. 52.   103. Ibid., p. 69.

104. Ibid., p. 72.   105. Ibid., p. 104.

106. Ibid., p. 121.   107. Ibid., p. 127.

108. Ibid., p. 129.   109. Ibid., p. 131.

110. Ibid.   111. Ibid., p. 137.

112. Ibid., pp. 201-202.   113. Ibid., p. 203.

114. Ibid., p. 215.

115. Letter, B. Harrison Decker to Edwin Lewis, 17 October 1934, ELC.

116. Letter, George B. Thomas to Edwin Lewis, 29 August 1934, ELC.

117. Letter, William F. Seitter to Edwin Lewis, 6 September 1934, ELC.

118. Letter, Clinton M. Cherry to Edwin Lewis, 26 September 1934, ELC.

119. Ibid.

120. Letter, Harold Paul Sloan to Edwin Lewis, 8 September 1934, ELC.

121. See The Christian Advocate 59 (September 20, 1934): 778; and (October 18, 1934): 850.

122. Letter, Norman W. Tiddy to Edwin Lewis, 23 September 1934, ELC.

123. These chapters, "The Foredoomed Man," "The Atoning Deed," and "The Incarnate God," are the ones in which Lewis outlined the essentials of the historic faith.

124. Letter, Norman Twiddy to Edwin Lewis, 23 September 1934, ELC.

125. Letter, John Versteeg to Edwin Lewis, no date, ELC.

126. Ibid.

127. Letter, Jonathan B. Hawk to Edwin Lewis, 16 October 1934, ELC.

128. The Christian Century 51 (November 7, 1934): 1416.

129. Francis J. McConnell, "A Christian Manifesto," Religion in Life 3 (Autumn 1934): 614-618.

130. Ibid., pp. 617-618.   131. Ibid., p. 618.

132. The Christian Advocate 109 (November 29, 1934): 962.

133. The Christian Advocate 109 (August 23, 1934): 708.

134. Ibid.

135. "From Philosophy to Revelation," p. 764.

136. Ibid.

137. "Three Representative Leaders in Contemporary American Methodist Theology," p. 185.

138. "The Rev. Edwin Lewis," The Teachers of Drew, James R. Joy, ed. (Madison N.J.: Drew

University Press, 1942), p. 144.

139. "From Liberalism to Neo-Orthodoxy: The History of a Theological Transition, 1925-1935" (Ph.D. diss., Harvard University, 1974). See also his brief synopsis, "The Emergence of American Neo-orthodoxy," Reformed Review 30 (Autumn 1976): 35-38.

140. The term "conversion" does not refer here to an initial religious experience, but to a change of mind. Failure to distinguish between these two meanings helped to create one of the "myths" that Lewis had been "converted," i.e. had an initial religious experience, later in life. As Carl Michalson points out, however, Lewis was "converted" in that sense during his boyhood through the influence of his Sunday School teacher. See Michalson, "The Edwin Lewis Myth," The Christian Century 77 (February 24, 1960): 218.

141. "From Liberalism to Neo-orthodoxy," p. 2.

142. "Continental Influence on American Christian Thought since World War I," Church History 27 (September 1958): 260.

143. "What the War Did to My Mind," p. 1161, quoted in Hutchison, The Modernist Impulse in American Protestantism, pp. 226-227.

144. "From Liberalism to Neo-orthodoxy," p. 205.

145. For a concise but thorough discussion of how Barth's theology came to America, and how it has influenced American theology, see Dennis Voskuil, "America Encounters Karl Barth," Fides et Historie 12 (Spring 1980): 61-74.

146. Douglas Horton, Foreward to Karl Barth, The Word of God and the Word of Man, trans. by Horton (New York: Harper and Row, 1957), pp. 1-2.

147. Edwin Lewis read The Word of God and the Word of Man in 1928. In 1932 he read Barth's Commentary on the Epistle to the Romans. See William B. Lewis, "The Role of Harold Paul Sloan and the Methodist League for Faith and Life in the Fundamentalist Modernist Controversy of the

Methodist Episcopal Church," p. 266.

148. The Modernist Impulse in American Protestantism, pp. 257-258.

149. See the discussion of Machen and Lippman in ibid., pp. 261-274.

150. "Impotent Liberalism," The Christian Century 43 (February 11, 1926): 167-168.

151. "The Sickness of Liberal Religion," The World Tomorrow 14 (August 1931): 256-259.

152. "After Liberalism -- What?," The Christian Century 50 (November 8, 1933): 1403-1406.

153. For a description of Niebuhr's critique see the chapter, "The Disillusioning of a Liberal," in Ronald H. Stone, Reinhold Niebuhr: Prophet to Politicians (Nashville: The Abingdon Press, 1972), pp. 35-53.

154. See especially Does Civilization Need Religion? (New York: The Macmillan Company, 1927); and "Let Liberal Churches Stop Fooling Themselves!," The Christian Century 48 (March 25, 1931): 402.

155. A Religious History of the American People (New Haven: Yale University Press, 1972), p. 941.

156. Ahlstrom designates 1934 as the annus mirabilis of the movement. See ibid., p. 943; and his "Continental Influence on American Thought Since World War I," pp. 265-267.

Chapter 3

THE DIVINE CHRIST

Re-enthroning Christ

In "The Fatal Apostasy of the Modern Church," Lewis had insisted that to be "saved," the modern church must "re-enthrone Christ,"[1] and in his Manifesto, that the "restoration of Christ to his rightful place" was the church's "urgent need."[2] This meant presenting Christ first and foremost as the Divine Word, the Eternal Son of God, God manifest in the flesh, and only then, as the historical Jesus, the Son of Man.[3] Thus in direct contrast to his earlier Christology, where he began with the human Christ, the starting-point for Lewis' Christology after 1933 was the divine Christ.

As a result, Christ could never be looked upon merely as a teacher who told humanity about God; He himself was God speaking. "His speech was the speech of God and his action the action of God."[4] Nor could he be merely one who with groping hands "reached up into the Infinite beyond and brought it down;"[5] He himself came from that beyond -- it was his eternal abode. In the face of the fact of Christ, God thus asks to recognize that "we are facing himself."[6] Moreover, we face God in Christ not because he attained the highest possible degree of God-consciousness, but because he actually possessed "the metaphysical status that belonged only to God."[7]

This belief, though expressed in various ways, has always persisted in the church, and is the "trunkline of clear Christological conviction running down the Christian centuries."[8] Yet surprisingly the modern church, in attempting to make the faith compatible with categories of modern thought, was willing to surrender it. According to those categories, only truths capable of being verified by scientific methods were acceptable; and those which could not be validated by such methods, regardless of their place in the New Testament or the history of Christianity, were set aside. As a result, a reduced conception of Christ emerged where Christ was looked upon not as the high point in God's quest for humanity, but as the high point in humanity's quest for God. Jesus revealed God

-- yes, but only to a greater degree than other men and women had revealed him. He was not, however, the self-revelation of God himself.

Such a view, Lewis maintained, was totally incompatible with that of the New Testament and the historic church:

> There are those who see Jesus as the Eternal Son of God in the flesh, who came among us to accomplish our deliverance from sin and death. There are others who see in Jesus a man of unusual religious insight, who had been enabled to discover the truth about God, man himself, the world, so that those who accept this truth are set free. These concepts are absolutely antithetical, not only for themselves but in all they imply.[9]

Acceptance of the modern church's liberal conception of Christ therefore means the loss of true knowledge of God. If Jesus is less than the Eternal Son of God, "the question of questions is still unanswered. We still do not know what God is, nor even _that_ He is."[10] The Christian religion, in turn, becomes another human aspiration, "a ladder set up on the earth, not a ladder let down from heaven."[11] The modern view also spells the doom for authentic Christian experience[12] and the Christian understanding of grace.[13]

When, therefore, the conviction that Jesus Christ is the Eternal Son of God was surrendered, much more was lost than a mere theological theory:

> What is lost? A Word of God in the form of a great act of God: a final Revelation of the nature and final results of sin; a moral dynamic equal to every Christian demand. And also the fullest significance of the Christian festivals, Christmas, Good Friday and Easter and Pentecost is lost. And the fullest significance of the great Christian ceremonies such as Baptism, the Lord's Supper, The Lamb, The Cross, and The Altar, are all lost.
>   The Modern Church will never recover that lost significance unless it recovers Jesus Christ as he confronts us in the New Testament.[14]

94

A Logos Christology

Out of his concern, then, to see the modern church "recover the Christocentric glory of the faith,"[15] Lewis formulated his doctrine of Christ. And although he never devoted a complete work to it as he had earlier, because of this concern, Christology continued to occupy a central place in his many and varied writings.

As John Sims suggests,[16] it can best be characterized as a Logos Christology, for repeatedly he identifies Christ with the Eternal Word of God:

> When we speak of the Divinity of Christ, applying the term to him considered as a historical figure, what we mean is the Divinity of the Word. In the same way, the eternity of Christ is the eternity of the Word; the power of Christ is the power of the Word.[17]

> The historical Jesus and the Risen Christ root in the one and the same ultimate fact -- the Eternal Word.[18]

Thus the concept of the Logos underlies Lewis' mature Christology and unites its various facets. In defining it he states:

> There is that in God which, as the ultimate determinant of his nature and of the form of his free activities, constitutes therefore the basis of both of his involution in the self-revealing and redemptive process. This is called variously the logos; the Word; an eternal divine "form"; the divine "self-image" which all things reflect and in which they cohere: the "Son" who eternally expresses God's substance.[19]

As Logos, Christ is "imminent and determinative in God,"[20] or as Lewis also expresses it, "intrinsic to the Divine Life."[21] This means that God cannot exist as a solitary or undifferentiated Being, but exists as a Fellowship. It also means that Lewis can affirm without hesitation something he could not affirm before, viz., the pre-existence of Christ:[22]

Let us say it very simply as a cardinal

Christian doctrine, that one who lived as a
Man among men -- namely, Jesus of Nazareth --
had, before he lived among men, shared in the
experience of God because he shared in the
essential nature, the eternal form of God.[23]

As Logos, Christ is also "imminent and
determinative" in creation. The Word "constitutes the
metaphysical basis" whereby the Divine Life "comes to
objective self-expression in creation as we know it."[24]
Thus the fact, the miracle, the the purpose of
creation, the glory of the Creator are all so
intertwined with the fact of Christ that "he becomes
the nexus without which none of these had been
possible."[25]

Human beings, as part of creation, in turn reflect
the divine Logos. Created in the image of God, their
very constitution is interwoven with "an element that
is an analogue"[26] to the Logos in God. Thus the Logos
provides the basis for the kinship between God and
humanity which makes God's self-revelation "susceptible
of being apprehended"[27] by humans.

The Centrality of the Incarnation

This divine self-revelation unfolds through a
progressive process which is also a progressive revelation of the Logos. The process begins with the primal
event of creation and culminates in an event of like
nature and significance: the incarnation of the Word
in the historical person of Jesus of Nazareth. In this
event God is absolutely and supremely self-disclosed:

Here we meet him in his living actuality.
Here we know what he is. The point where the
Creator appears as an intrinsic part of his
own creation . . . No longer is it necessary
to move precariously and uncertainly from the
act to the Actor, saying, "Because God does
this, he must be that." Rather we can say,
"Here the Act and the Actor are identities.
This is not simply something that God does:
this is what God is. The succession of
"mighty acts" of a veiled God, evoking the
response of faith, is consummated in the
"Mighty Fact" of a God unveiled, at once
faith's confirmation and its all-sufficient
justification.
This point is known as the incarnation

of the Eternal Son of the Eternal Father . .
. The Word . . . here "becomes flesh."[28]

Yet as the focal point of God's self-revelation,
the incarnation must not be conceived as un upward
movement of humanity toward God, but as a downward
movement of God toward humanity. It is therefore not
"the supreme upreach of man's unavailing hands toward
the unknown and unknowable God," but "the supreme
downreach toward man of the redeeming hands of the
self-revealing God."[29] Only when it is viewed in this
way -- the divine descending to the human, not the
human ascending to the divine -- does the incarnation
have determinative and absolute significance:

> "For us men he came down." We do not
> like to say it, because we have been trained
> in a point of view which sees only a "coming
> up." What comes up has only a relative
> significance, and we can handle it -- or we
> think we can. But what comes down is against
> the rule. It violates the order of things.
> It suggests the possibility that this is a
> lower realm under the control of a higher
> realm. It threatens us with an absolute. So
> we will have nothing to do with one who "came
> down," . . .
> Yet the refusal only deepens our
> darkness and increases our perplexity because
> it leaves us without linkage to a greater
> than we are ourselves . . . For who can lift
> us except be he above us, and how can he lift
> us except he connect with us?[30]

Yet what is it that makes this "coming down"
possible? Why is God able to "connect with us"? In
answering this extremely important question Lewis
points to the two necessary preconditions for the
incarnation.[31] The first lies in the divine nature
which is constituted not as monad, but as Trinity. As
Lewis explains it, to have a human experience the
divine being must be able to add a human form to the
divine form. But then he asks,

> Would this addition be even possible were it
> not for the prior fact that God is so
> constituted that his form is shared, and that
> one of the sharing constituents is of such a
> character, is so dependently related to the
> will of the other, that it is at this point

that the addition of the human form to the divine form is already provided for?[32]

Lewis admits that because of problems inherent in the doctrine of the Trinity, there had been a time when he felt "a curious antipathy to the idea."[33] But he had come to see the wisdom of the historic church in adhering to the doctrine for it provides the necessary basis for faith in a real incarnation.[34] He therefore concludes, "There could be Incarnation because in God's very nature from all eternity there had been sonship just as much as there had been Fatherhood."[35]

The second precondition for the Incarnation lies in the nature of humanity. God can confront "only a creature whose structure is such that he can recognize the confrontation."[36] Such a structure within humans enabling them to receive and comprehend the meaning of revelation is therefore "axiomatic" if there is to be a genuine incarnation.[37] Unlike divine incarnations in religions such as Hinduism, God cannot be incarnated in a monkey or an elephant since animals such as these cannot adequately receive or interpret revelation. What, however, is necessary, has been provided in the very constitution of human beings. They can both "hear" and "interpret" the Word of God.[38]

Incarnation, then, is possible because both God and humans are constituted as they are. And as we have already noted, it is the Logos as imminent and determinative in both, which establishes the essential kinship between them.

But the incarnation is not only possible: it is actual in the form of a real historical event. "What God did in Christ he did in the same stream of history within which all his other activities fell."[39] For the Christian faith to be valid, Lewis thus believed it must be grounded in relevant facts. Moreover, he was unwilling to "bifurcate truths and ideas from facts and events"[40] or to treat facts in a symbolic way. Convinced that such attempts to resolve the tension between faith and historical science involved a direct attack upon the historical bases of the faith, he thus states emphatically:

> Abandoning the factual means abandoning the historical, and the very thing that makes Christianity so significant is just the startling events through which it was

created. Hegel notwithstanding, there is all the difference in the world between an actual historical Incarnation and the mere God-man idea as the synthesizing of the two opposite ideas of God and Man.[41]

At the same time, however, Lewis was just as emphatic that although the Incarnation was a real historical event, it could not be contained within historical categories. Something had happened in Jesus Christ which was utterly unique. Though he had historical antecedents, "something new appears with him, so new that it has no historical antecedents to account for it."[42] The Incarnation is therefore "an irruption, a discontinuity,"[43] which defies historical explanation. It is an event which is as original and unique as the primal event of creation itself:

> That series of episodes, therefore, which marks the presence of Christ in the field of history is as inexplicable in terms of the processes of that history as the primal creative act is inexplicable in terms of the processes which characterize creation in its ongoing . . . In both cases, we have an absolute which is to be accepted as utterly original.[44]

The Incarnation, then, is a miraculous event, "as truly miraculous as that primal volition of the Creator,"[45] and as such, an event which we "can only call 'supernatural.'"[46] It is not, however, to be viewed as one miracle among others, but as the primary miracle, the supreme miracle, which "carries with it, by the sheer force of the law of congruity, every other miracle."[47] As the primary miracle, the Incarnation "gives versimilitude" to the other miracles; once it has been accepted the others "take on a certain inevitability."[48]

The healing miracles of Christ are therefore acts congruous with his Person. The same also applies to those "veritable stones of offense," the Virgin Birth and the Resurrection, and justifies what Lewis calls "the supreme acquiescence."[49] Even these "cease to be a problem, because all appear as integral parts of that self-consistent whole of truth and reality which is constituted of the Incarnation of the Son of God."[50]

Against those who maintain that the Virgin Birth

and the Resurrection must either be rejected or
reinterpreted to make the faith credible to the
scientific mind, Lewis contends that these elements do
not not need scientific corroboration to be accepted
any more than the doctrine of the Trinity or the
Incarnation since they too lie outside the realm of
science and in the realm of faith.[51] Arguments, then,
from the physical or natural sciences are bound to be
irrelevant. "Faith is never asked to consider the
Birth of Christ as primarily a biological phenomenon.
Instead what is offered is offered as sheer miracle."[52]
Likewise, with regard to the resurrection, "We are
asked to believe in it, not as a possibility in the
order of nature, but as an impossibility in that order
as constituted, and yet as an event which actually
occurred and which could only occur because the subject
of it was nature's Lord."[53] This, then, was how Lewis
dealt with the problems of science and history in
justifying his "acquiescence."

However, his chief rationale for the
"acquiescence" was, as has already been stated, that
these events were vital parts of the whole Christian
truth, and therefore could not be surrendered without
having a profound effect upon the whole. Thus while
admitting that the scriptural accounts of the Virgin
Birth and the Resurrection may leave us with many
unsolved problems, Lewis is still confident that one
can say,

> Nevertheless, I believe, and I believe
> primarily because of the intrinsic nature of
> Christianity; because ultimately it must
> stand or fall as an organic whole; because
> part fits into part with an astonishing
> exactitude; and because when the living whole
> is disintegrated, the fragments that are
> left, useful though they may still be, and
> acceptable for certain purposes, lack not
> only the intellectual cogency of the whole,
> but also, and more seriously, its moral power
> and its spiritual majesty.[54]

For Lewis, the vital center of that organic whole
is the doctrine of the Incarnation. Thus he questions
whether the fundamental difficulty for those who are
hesitant in affirming the Virgin Birth and the
Resurrection is really with those elements at all, but
with the Incarnation itself. He wonders whether they
are first letting go of these two constituent parts

because they actually wish to abandon the whole.

In discussing these events, it is therefore typical of Lewis to first establish the validity of the Incarnation. In reference to the Virgin Birth, for example, he refuses to build the case for the deity of Christ on his miraculous birth:

> To accept the miracle that is Jesus on the prior ground of the miracle of his birth is to reverse the order of faith . . . The miracle of the birth, which was historically first, appeared nevertheless as the capstone of faith and not its foundation.[55]

Likewise, with regard to the resurrection, he insists that only one thing makes it credible:

> . . . the fact that the subject of it was the Eternal Son of God . . . The Incarnation, therefore, is the fundamental miracle. When Jesus Christ is seen as God-become-man, the Resurrection is no longer an irrationability. Instead it becomes the supremely rational event of human history . . .[56]

His argument, then, is that the Incarnation, along with these events, the Virgin Birth and the Resurrection, stand or fall together. "If we are to have these we must have him, and we must have him as in the faith of the Church he has always been held to be -- the Son of God Incarnate. But if we do have him, then we can have these too."[57]

As the culmination and focal point of God's self-revelation, the Incarnation stands as an absolute and final event. God has spoken in a Son so that no other word is needed "except to enforce and apply this one ultimate speech."[58] In the Incarnation, then, the meaning of all things is ultimately revealed, including the nature and purpose of God, creation, humanity and history.[59] All things are therefore "constituted with reference to Christ."[60] In him they "find their coherence."[61] He is "cosmic root, cosmic nexus, cosmic crown."[62]

It was this deep-seated conviction which produced the New Testament, and prior to that, produced the church whose testimony the New Testament contains.[63] The modern church failed to properly understand this and thus sought to separate the Christ of this conviction, i.e., the Christ of faith, from the historical figure of Jesus of Nazareth, i.e., the Jesus of history. The latter, it was argued, was a real historical figure, while the former was a supernatural and therefore imaginary one which was later imposed upon the latter. As a result the Christ of faith had colored the accounts of the Jesus of history. This coloring was most noticeable in certain places such as the birth narratives, the descriptions of the healing miracles, and the resurrection narratives. The job, then, of criticism, was to remove the coloring so that a truer, more historical picture of Christ could be retained.

What was overlooked, however, was that all our records of the historical Jesus were given to us by men and women who had already arrived at a conviction about Jesus which "set him at the very center of divine-human relations."[64] Thus from the very beginning, the Jesus of history was interpreted from the perspective of the Christ of faith, and not the other way around.[65] To start, then, with the Jesus of history reverses the proper procedure. "It is wrong historically; it is wrong in the perspective of faith itself."[66] Of the two sides, the faith side and the account side, the former is primary, not the latter.[67] Yet although the two sides can be distinguished, they cannot be separated:

> The Jesus of history was not destroyed by the Christ of faith. The two are one and the same. The first led to the second, but the second was the crown and consummation of the first. The attempt to separate the Jesus of history and the Christ of faith is therefore an attempt to divide the indivisible. What God has made one, let not man regard as two.[68]

The Humanity of Christ

There were, of course, those who argued that this approach, which begins with the Christ of faith rather than the Jesus of history, inevitably results in a docetic Christology. Lewis, however, believed that such need not necessarily follow. To begin with the lesser (the Jesus of history) excludes the greater (the Christ of faith), but one can begin with the greater and still include the lesser.[69] After all, it is precisely the fact that Christ is divinely significant that makes him humanly significant as well. As "Very Man" he "discloses forever why God made every other man, and what God desires every other man at last to be."[70] Thus although the affirmation of the divinity of Christ is the dominate note in Lewis' Christology he continues to stress, as he had earlier, his full humanity too:

> Not only is he the Word of God become flesh -- the living actuality of what is most truly and most deeply the divine -- but he is the supreme Act of God. Yet this man, who has this significance, who carries the key which unlocks the door by which God and men are kept apart, is so completely a man that if there is one thing more than another that stands out in the Gospel story it is the utter humanness of his experience. From his birth to his death, he is "like unto his brethren." He is nowhere represented as an excrescence on the race. He is no interloper, no pretender. He is literally bone of our bone and flesh of our flesh. In the most complete sense, he knew the human lot.[71]

But _how_ did the Eternal Word become a fully human being? In answering that question Lewis relies heavily upon the kenotic theory,[72] a theory which, as we have noted above,[73] he previously rejected. In becoming a human being the Eternal Son therefore emptied himself. This self-emptying, however, did not involve a change in the divine _morphe_, i.e., his essential divine nature, but a change in the divine _schema_, i.e., the conditions under which his life was lived. The Eternal Son thus exchanged the "milieu of God" for the "milieu of man":

> The Son gave up the conditions of Deity for the conditions of humanity, the experience of the common glory of the divine for the experience of the servitude and subjection of the human . . . The contrast, therefore, is not the contrast between being the Son of God and being a man: the contrast is between life according to the divine fashion or style and life according to the human fashion or style.[74]

The result is nonetheless a real humiliation and human experience while the divine morphe "retains an unbroken continuity."[75] Lewis notes that historically this was one of the major reasons why the church attached significance to the virgin birth: because it secures the continuity between the incarnate Christ and the Godhead. It also means that Christ did not come out of history, but into history out of the being of God.[76]

As the Incarnate Son, however, Christ's response to the Father's will is now made under human conditions, and thus takes on an ethical significance it never had before. Now there is the possibility of uncertainty concerning the Father's will; now there is the possibility of misunderstanding it; now there is the possibility of hesitating, yes even refusing to submit to it. Thus the Father's will "became for the Son of God in the flesh what it had never been for the Son of God not yet in the flesh -- a problem."[77]

For Lewis, only if this is the case can there be a true incarnation and a fully human Christ. "How can we call a being made in our likeness a man if the will of God is never to him a problem but always something perfectly evident and always something unhesitatingly accepted?"[78] He is therefore critical of Christologies which, in attempting to explain the divine-human synthesis of the Incarnation, stress the divine nature of Christ at the expense of the human. In discussing Appolinarius, for example, he notes that in his bold attempt to avoid the prevalent dualistic tendencies of Christology during his period he succeeded, "but only at the expense of making the human unreal." By his very own definition, Appolinarius "left out what was most truly human, fallible human reason, and fallible moral will."[79] He also noted a similar deficiency in the Christology of Thomas Aquinas. Bound by his metaphysical principles, divinity, for him, meant that Christ had to possess divine attributes. Thus because he was divine he was therefore omniscient; and because he was omniscient he was perfect in knowledge from the moment of conception.[80]

Lewis, however, rejects any such attempts to posit divine attributes to the Incarnate Christ because he believed that possession of such attributes was incompatible with his full humanity: "Humanity and omniscience; humanity and omnipotence; humanity and independence of space and time; humanity and freedom from all pain, effort, and temptation -- these are not

104

only incompatibilities: they are flat contradictions."[81] As a part of his own presentation of the humanity of Christ, Lewis laid great stress on the growing messianic consciousness of Jesus and described in considerable detail what was involved in the process.[82] It began, he believed, during the "silent years" of his boyhood and youth when Jesus "came to feel himself marked for some high service,"[83] service somehow related to the work of the proclaimed messiah. This explains why he joined the movement headed by John the Baptist, and why he asked John to baptize him.[84] It was during his baptism that God first revealed to him that he himself was to be the messiah: "In that moment, something happens in the soul of Jesus. Vague intimations come to some clarification. The conviction springs to birth in him irresistably, that he is to be the long-promised Deliverer of his people."[85]

The temptation which followed was "the proper consequence"[86] of this revelation. Jesus had to find out what the Kingdom of God meant, and his encounter with Satan was the first part of that process: finding out what it did not mean. The Kingdom he would establish would not be based upon political reform, miracle working, or an empire built on force. Thus when he left the wilderness to begin his public ministry, "He only knew what the kingdom was not. He did not yet know what it was."[87]

The early part of his ministry centered around his preaching, teaching and healing, and was marked by great optimism. During this time Jesus himself was under the influence of the prevailing apocalyptic conception of the Kingdom. According to that conception, the Kingdom would be ushered in on the Day of the Lord when, accompanied by signs and wonders, God would destroy the wicked and set up a new order. Prior to that day, the messiah would have arrived and would be preparing his faithful followers for it. All the followers would, of course, be Israelites since the Kingdom was reserved exclusively for them.

That Jesus was in fact acting under the influence of this conception is evident in the instructions he gave to the Twelve when he sent them out to preach. They were to limit their ministry to the house of Isreal, and to prepare themselves for the coming of the Son of man who would appear before they had completed their mission. Meanwhile, Jesus went away "to wait the coming revelation of divine power -- the sudden appearing from heaven of the kingdom of God."[88]

However the expected Parousia did not occur; and so shortly thereafter, a disillusioned Jesus left his native land and travelled to Syro-Phoenicia in order to reconsider the nature of his messiahship. It was there through his epochal encounter with a Gentile woman that it dawned upon him that his mission was to all persons, and that the Kingdom of God had no boundaries. Thus the man who had entered Syro-Phoenicia as a nationalist, left as a universalist.[89]

That a definite change had taken place in Jesus is evident in that when he returned, he did not go directly to Galilee, but first visited the non-Jewish Decapolis to minister to people that before he would have passed by. While he was there his mind was opened to the scriptures, and he was drawn to Isaiah's description of the Suffering Servant. He became haunted by that description, and could not resist applying it to himself and his mission as the messiah:

> This is what it means to be the Messiah: this is what Messiah must do; this is the way Messiah must do it; this pouring out his soul unto death, this bearing the sin of many, this becoming an offering for sin, is the burden laid upon Messiah.[90]

Shortly thereafter at Caesarea-Philippi, Jesus first expressed his new understanding of messiahship in "one of the most epochal conversations of history."[91] In answer to his question, "Who do men say that I am?" Peter had confessed, "Thou art the Christ"; and Jesus had accepted his reply. But to Peter and the other disciples' total amazement and utter consternation, he immediately began to speak of his impending suffering and death:

> Not a crown but a cross, not pomp and splendor but the shame and degradation that comes from self-forgetting love. He who suffers most is he who serves most; it is the cross that leads to the crown. There is no <u>anabasis</u> without a <u>katabasis</u>! No <u>plerosis</u> without a <u>kenosis</u>![92]

The transfiguration which followed, confirmed Jesus' new understanding of messiahship and encouraged him in the path he had chosen. Thus two seemingly antithetical ideas, the apocalyptic Son of Man and the Suffering Servant of God were "brought together in the mind of Jesus, and completely fused as mutualities."[93] He who would be the one, he had come to believe, must also be the other.

This, according to Lewis, was the quintessence of the messianic consciousness of Jesus;[94] and the fact that he only came to this understanding over a period of time was essential if his full humanity was to be maintained. As a man he possessed a fallible human reason which therefore meant the necessity of growth in his understanding.

Along the very same lines, Lewis also stressed the reality of Christ's moral trial. As a man Christ possessed a fallible moral will. Thus as he faced each moral choice, "the possibility of failure was implicit in the situation, just as it was in the drama of the Garden of Eden."[95] His temptations, then, were in no way artificial, but real.

There were, however, those who argued that this affirmation -- that Christ's temptations were real -- and the affirmation that he was sinless, which Lewis also maintained, were incompatible with each other. To say that Christ was sinless, and sinless because he was divine, was to place his temptations in a different category than ours and therefore make them meaningless to us. Lewis, however, insisted that the very opposite was true:

> He can still mean very much to us. Indeed, his meaning is largely in the very fact of his sinlessness! His sinlessness does not mean that he was above temptation. Temptation does not take the same forms. One person is tempted in one way; another person in another way. The temptations of Jesus Christ were temptations which went with his being who he was.
> But while the forms of temptation differ, its essence is always the same: it is in a felt pressure to depart from what is believed to be the will of God. Jesus knew that pressure as any other man knows it, and he resisted it, not automatically, but by an effort -- even on one occasion to "sweating as it were great drops of blood." It was

costly obedience -- "obedience even unto the death of the Cross."[96]

In every respect, then, the experience of the Eternal Word become flesh in the historical person of Jesus of Nazareth was fully human.   There was the normal human pattern: birth, infancy, childhood, youth, adulthood, and yes, even death.   There was growth in knowledge and understanding in keeping with normal human mental limitations and the limitations of a particular time and culture.   There was genuine temptation with real possibility of failure.   There was involvement in all the normal processes such as hunger, thirst, pain, weariness, work, rest, companionship, moral struggle, faith, and religious aspiration.[97] There was the experiencing of the full range of human emotions including loneliness, disappointment, fear, anger, joy, and exhilarition. When, therefore, the Son of God "took on the human form and entered into the servile human fashion, he became 'in all things . . . like unto his brethren.'"[98]

The Meaning of the Incarnation

Thus Lewis, as he had in his earlier Christology, is determined to establish the full humanity of Christ. However, his reason for doing so is quite different now.   In his earlier Christology he had stressed his humanity in order to safeguard his moral achievement. Only if what Christ achieved, viz., an absolute God-consciousness, was achieved by one who was fully human could it have significance for men and women.   Now, in direct contrast, he stresses Christ's humanity for the opposite reason: to safeguard the divine achievement, viz., God achieving an absolute human consciousness.[99] Only if Christ is fully human can we be sure that God has really experienced and therefore fully understands the human lot.

For the mature Lewis, then, the meaning of the incarnation is just the opposite of what it was before. Before it was humanity knowing the experience of God: " . . . in Jesus Christ we meet one who thought as God thought, who acted as God acted, who suffered as God suffered, and who therefore, in his thought and action and suffering . . . is the incarnation of God."[100] But now it is God knowing the experience of humanity:[101]

The very things from which of right God is exempt -- ignorance, pain, temptation, weariness, disappointment, the agony of fear, even dark and dreadful death -- he knows as really as we know them, and in the same way that we know them. God invaded the human, yes! but he invaded the human by allowing the human to invade him.[102]

The fact and the meaning of humanity has thus been taken up into the very structure of divinity. The Incarnate Son, by reason of his metaphysical status, "transfers moment by moment into the very heart of Deity every single experience he has."[103] The incarnation has therefore "humanized the Godhead."[104] The ontological distinction between the divine and the human "has become an ontological identity."[105]

For Lewis this involves a structural modification,[106] a "radical disruption"[107] of the internal relations within the Godhead. Thus the incarnation has profoundly affected God. God "suffered the shock of self-mutilation"[108] through the admission of "an alien element"[109] into his being. And as a result, "the inner structure and experience of the Absolute, supposedly a fixed quantum, has suffered a change."[110]

Lewis, of course, realizes that there are metaphysical objections to such a position. Above all, it challenges the assumption of theistic absolutism that since God is impassible he can never undergo any type of modification or be involved in any new experience.[111] Such objections, however, at best are only speculative; moreover, they rob us of the mystery of the redemptive love of God in Christ because they "do not frankly recognize the tragic note in the experience of God"[112] which was caused by the incarnation. By insisting, then, that the incarnation had an ontological effect upon God the costliness of redemptive love is dramatized and revealed:

> The Infinite Mystery is in the fact that when divine love goes to its redeeming uttermost, it does so by enduring a radical disruption of the internal relations in which is its perfect blessedness. Logos incarnation in the human, to constitute the means of redemption by first securing a Redeemer, is not merely a piece of divine routine. It is sacrificial action which, while not disrupting the divine fellowship,

introduces into it a tragic note, indicated as to its ultimate poignancy by the cry of dereliction from the cross. By nothing less than this could the full measure of the holy love of God be disclosed.[113]

In stating that this disruption of the internal relations of the Godhead does not disrupt the divine fellowship, Lewis wants to make it clear that the material of God's being was not altered by the incarnation; rather, it was the pattern which was altered.[114] He describes this alteration in pattern like this:

> There was a time when he did not know creatureliness, and now he does know it. Once he did not know opposition to his will, and now he does. Once he did not know the meaning of pain (as God, could he?), and now he does. Once he did not know the sense of utter futility, and now he does. Once he did not know that awful moment when the soul feels the whole universe slipping away from it -- "and after that the dark" -- and now he does. And he knows it not by mere sympathetic imagination -- he may be supposed always to have done that -- but by personal participation.[115]

Finally, Lewis insists that this ontological alteration in the being of God affected by the incarnation is not temporary, but remains as a permanent fact of existence.[116] It was because he denied this that Lewis was critical of Origen's Christology. In his doctrine of the incarnation, there is no real union of the divine and the human, but only a temporary use of the human by the divine. As a result, the incarnation was "merely an episode, and that's all. All is as it was before."[117]

For Lewis, however, because of the incarnation, all is not the same, nor will it ever be. "'The Word became flesh,' and never again can the Word just be the Word. The fleshly limitations are no longer there, but what happened to the Word because of the acceptance of those limitations is permanent."[118] In reaching down to sinful humanity, God is thus left with an eternal scar, "for the throne of God is the throne of God and of the Lamb, 'the Lamb that hath been slain.'"[119]

The Nature of the Atonement

Reference to the scar and the slain lamb leads us to Lewis' conception of the work of Christ, and particularly his doctrine of atonement. Here he is emphatic that the discussion must begin, not with the need of humanity, but with the nature of God, and specifically with that which is central to his character, viz., his holiness. Once this is granted, he maintains, the rest of the doctrine falls into place.[120] The modern church with its sentimentalized conception of God[121] failed to sufficiently take God's holiness into account. The result was a subjective understanding of the atonement which robbed the work of Christ of its efficacy and its power. In order, then, to properly secure the doctrine and to guard against the modern error, Lewis goes so far as to say: "The evangelical view of God, first and foremost is not that he is a loving Father, tender and compassionate and merciful, but that he is holy."[122]

The corollary of this conviction is that human beings are sinful. The order, moreover, is significant. The nature of divine holiness determines the nature of human sinfulness, and not vice versa:

> Always, therefore, over against sin stands a prior holiness -- God. That holiness is not only a priority in point of time: it is also an ultimate, an absolute. If there is to be a holiness in time, it can be only on the condition that there is an eternal holiness. It is that holiness that makes sin to be sin: otherwise, while we might still characterize it as an incident of growth, experimentation, unsociability, even missing the mark, we could not speak of it as sin in the sense of a fatal culpability -- which is what sin is, since God is the Holy One.[123]

In describing the nature of this "fatal culpability" Lewis stresses that it is not merely the sum total of sinful acts, but extends beyond acts to a fundamental dislocation in human nature. Sin is therefore both a status and a deed and although the acts confirm the status, the status always antedates the deed.[124] Sinful acts thus grow out of a prior sinful nature, a nature which they reveal as "chaotic and disorganized."[125]

As a result of sin, there is enmity between God and humanity:

> The holy God and the sinful man stand over against each other -- opposites: not simply because the man has done certain specific sinful deeds, but just because the man is a man -- a born sinner, a member of the sinful race not by virtue of deliberate choice merely, but of necessity. He inherits a nature which assures his condemnation by the God from whom, in indirect and roundabout ways to be sure, his nature is received.[126]

As sinners, human beings thus stand under divine condemnation and are the objects of divine wrath. This wrath is God's steady purpose to destroy whatever opposes his love and contradicts his will.[127] Its ultimate expression is physical death. "We are mortal because we are sinful."[128] And although as their creator it was God's sovereign right to cause humans to be mortal, now because of their sinfulness, it is his obligation. "Even God is under the constraint of a 'must,' the must of his own holiness."[129]

But having created humans by choice, and condemned them by necessity, God is capable of going a step farther: he can deliver them from the condition which demands condemnation.[130] In his graciousness, this is precisely what he has done through the atonement wrought through Jesus Christ. "Of his Sovereign Will he made me. Of his Holy Necessity he condemned me. Of his Gracious Love he redeemed me."[131]

God, however, was not compelled to act graciously. What he did in Christ, he did not out of necessity but of his own choice. Grace, which was the divine motive for the atonement, is therefore "not an essential constituent of holiness,"[132] otherwise it would not be grace. The reason, then, that "the Creative God is the Atoning God" is because "besides being the Holy God he is also the Gracious God. But he is one God."[133] This, however, does not mean that grace is the consequence of the atonement; it is rather its fundamental cause. All along God desired to be gracious, but there were two barriers preventing the full exercise of his grace which had to be dealt with: the barrier from the side of his holiness, and the barrier from the side of human sinfulness. It was through the process of atonement that God removed these two barriers.

The first step in that process was the incarnation itself.[134]   In the person of Jesus Christ God crossed the line that separates Creator from creature:

> Absolute holiness . . . established itself within the stream of sinful and perishing humanity.   It was the most utterly sacrificial deed of which the Creator was capable: it was the cost of satisfying and revealing his own holiness and of making possible the exercise of his grace.[135]

By exchanging the divine form of existence for the human,   God in Christ thus endured a state of humiliation and self-deprivation which was essential if atonement was to be made.

The   entire   life of Christ was also part of the process of atonement since it was an expression of perfect obedience to the Father's will. As has already been noted,[136] the fact that it was obedience rendered within the human context charged it with ethical significance it never had when it was obedience rendered within the context of the divine life.   As a human   being,   his obedience was no longer "the unquestioning echo of the Eternal Father's will,"[137] but was obedience rendered in the face of all the human fallibilities.   Yet it was this crucial difference which makes it significant for us:

> . . . because it was perfect obedience under human conditions,   it was obedience having a redemptive power,   a possibility of vicarious imputation,   a range of social permeation operating through the humble gratitude of believing men who see this obedience rendered "in   our   behalf" that never could have attached to the untested obedience of the Eternal Son quiescent in the divine glory.[138]

This   process of atonement culminated in Christ's ultimate act of obedience: his death on the cross. Here where he "obeyed to the last dreadful limit,"[139] we move from an act of spontaneous obedience outside history   -- "he emptied himself" -- to an act of agonizing obedience within history -- "even unto death on a cross."

Yet it was not the physical pain he endured nor even the experience of physical death itself that constituted the supreme agony of the cross. It was the fact that on the cross he was abandoned by God:

> On the Cross, the world began to slip away from Him, and the faces of men began to slip away. That was the order of things, and, so God the Father were left to Him, it could be endured. But not thus was the cup drained. <u>God the Father also slipped away</u>. The cry was the cry of a broken heart: "Why has <u>thou</u> -- thou -- forsaken me --<u>me</u>!"[140]

But for atonement to be made it could not have been otherwise. For sin at its ultimate point is separation from God.[141] On the Cross, therefore, Jesus Christ stood in our place and endured that separation. In doing so he brought the tragedy of sin into the divine life itself: it was "the darkest hour in the experience of God."[142] Yet it was also the supreme revelation and expression of that which is deepest in God: holy love.[143] Divine holiness was passing its ultimate judgment upon sin, while divine love was ultimately being revealed. Thus wrath and love were conjoined in "one ultimate and complete expression":[144]

> The absolute of righteousness and the absolute of mercy co-exist at the cross conceived as the disclosure of the absolute of Holy Love . . . the Incarnate Son enduring the tragedy of the cross is judgment -- judgment pronounced by holiness and endured by holiness. But the cross is judgment that there might be deliverance . . .
> In a word, the cross, as the climactic point in the self-disclosure of God by the incarnation of the eternal Son and as the point where sin and holiness are at the death grapple, means that God is such a God as that his ultimate deed of judgment is at the same time his ultimate deed of love.[145]

But the process of atonement is not complete without the triumph of the resurrection. Without Easter, Good Friday is meaningless; therefore, the two must always be held together:

> Christianity stripped of the Risen and Living Christ is an impotent torso. Nothing but the

> Resurrection transforms the tragedy of
> Calvary into the nexus around which there
> swings, in an orbit whose full limits we are
> not able to trace, the vast redemptive
> purpose of the creative God.[146]

The resurrection thus means that God has triumphed over
sin, taken away the sting of the last enemy -- death,
and declared that good not evil has the last word. It
is God's answer to every question concerning the
finality of his holy love, and the sufficient ground
for trusting in that finality.

Through the process of atonement, God in Christ
has therefore done all that is necessary to remove the
barriers which prevented the full exercise of his
grace. However, we have discussed the atonement only
in relation to one of those barriers: the barrier on
the side of divine holiness. What, then, can we say
about the other barrier: the barrier on the side of
human sinfulness? How does the atonement affect it?
Does it not remain since men and women are still
sinners?

Lewis insists that the same means of atonement
which removed the barrier from the divine side is
sufficient to remove the barrier from the human side as
well. This latter barrier is not, however, removed
automatically. Men and women are not reconciled to God
simply because Christ died. The removal of the barrier
on the human side is conditioned upon a response of
faith, a response which in turn is possible only
because of God working in us. Through faith in Christ,
then, men and women are identified with the One who has
already identified with them. In doing so they obtain
from him that which he has made it possible for them to
receive:

> The repentant and believing and trusting soul
> acquires a new status: it changes unholiness
> for holiness. It passes from death unto
> life. It steps out from under the curse of
> its own necessary creaturehood. It is born
> again . . . The soul has found the ground of
> its forgiveness, the unfailing source of
> power, the all-sufficient motive to complete
> obedience. Christ "for me" becomes Christ
> "in me."[147]

Continuity and Discontinuity in
Lewis' Christology

These then are the main lines of the Christology which Lewis formulated from 1934 to the end of his career. His transition "from monism to dualism" which will be discussed in the next chapter, did have an effect on his Christology but that will be outlined later in conjunction with the transition. What we will see there, however, will not be a radical break or a complete change in Christological method as was the case in the earlier transition, "from philosophy to revelation." Rather we will note a shift of emphasis, a different focus, while his basic underlying approach remains the same.

Thus there is an essential continuity between the Christology presented in this chapter and the Christological emphases which grew out of Lewis' eventual adoption of a metaphysical dualism. In presenting Lewis' mature Christology we have therefore often cited sources which follow his formal acceptance of dualism in 1948; and later, in discussing the effect of that dualism upon his Christology, we will often cite sources which precede that date. By doing so we would emphasize that the two are not separate Christologies. The later emphases are instead an integral part of the Christology which has been presented here; so much so, that although our choosing to discuss them later is in keeping with the purpose of our study, it makes our presentation here incomplete.

The same, however, cannot be said when we compare Lewis' mature Christology to the Christology found in Jesus Christ and the Human Quest. Although there are elements of continuity between them, the elements of discontinuity outweigh them so much that the change must be characterized as radical. Whereas before his Christology was essentially a Christology from below; now it is a Christology from above. Whereas before his point of departure was the human Christ; now it is unequivocally the divine Christ. Whereas before he began with the work of Christ and then turned to questions concerning his person, now he begins with his person, and only after settling the question of who Christ is, is he interested in discussing what he did. Whereas before the essence of the incarnation was humanity experiencing divinity, now it is exactly the opposite: divinity experiencing humanity. Whereas before he had rejected the kenotic theory of how God became human, now he adopts that very theory. Whereas before he advocated a subjective, moral influence theory of the atonement, now he presents an objective, satisfaction theory. Whereas before the primary significance of the atonement was seen in its effect in producing an adequate repentance in humans, now its primary significance is seen in its removing the obstacles which separate God and humanity and which prevent the full expression of divine grace. Thus in almost all its major emphases, his mature Christology is radically different from the Christology he had formulated eariler.

Lewis and Bruner

In comparison with the Christologies being advanced by other theologians during this period, there are definite similarities between Lewis and Emil Brunner, particularly in their conceptions of the incarnation. Lewis always felt closer to Brunner than to Karl Barth, particularly the Brunner of The Mediator and Revelation and Reason.[148] Had he not been persuaded to circle the globe on behalf of Christiam missions, he would have spent the year, 1936, in Zurich studying with Brunner.[149]

Like Lewis, Brunner develops a Logos Christology. In fact, according to Lewis, it is when Brunner is discussing this subject, viz., the relation of the Eternal Word to the revelation of God in Christ, that he is at his best.[150] Concerning that relationship Brunner states: "Jesus is the Logos. He is the Word God has to speak to us . . . Jesus Christ is . . . an act of God, the self-manifestation of God, the final culmination of all the acts of revelation . . . the highest, personal, peculiar Word of God."[151] Brunner, then, conceives of the incarnation, not as the upward movement of humanity toward God, but as the downward movement of God toward humanity. "The central truth of the Christian faith is this: that the Eternal Son of God took upon Himself our humanity, not that the man Jesus acquired divinity."[152]

Like Lewis, he also presents the incarnation as an absolutely unique and therefore decisive event. Although it breaks into the sphere of the temporal, it is eternal; although it is truly historical, it transcends history.[153] As such it is an event which the historian, merely as a historian cannot fully comprehend. Faith alone can grasp the super-historical significance in and behind the historical event.[154]

Faith, then, "believes in a Christ who from the point of view of historical science, must always remain an unsolved problem, a Christ whose bare existence may even be called into question."[155] Yet though historical science may assault faith, it can never really refute it because it is based not on historical science, but on the self-authenticating word of revelation.

The Criticism of Niebuhr and Others

It was, however, his agreement with Brunner at this particular point, viz., that the incarnation as a fact of revelation was inaccessible to historical science, that caused Lewis to be severely criticized. For example, in his critical review of A Philosophy of the Christian Revelation, J.S. Bixler stated:

> We may agree that religion is neither philosophy or science. But this is not to say that its special dogmas are beyond criticism from biology or history . . . when we lay claim to knowledge of events in nature or history we cannot avoid submitting our beliefs to all the tests which have been devised.[156]

Likewise, George W. Davis faulted Lewis for taking refuge in the half-truth that truths such as the incarnation are not truths of reason, but truths of faith.[157] And Edward T. Ramsdell of Vanderbilt noted his "unresolved confusion" in that having recognized the value of human criteria as valid for discovering revelation in other areas, "Dr. Lewis insists that the ultimate revelation of God in Christ cannot be judged by 'human' criteria but must be accepted purely on faith as a gift of God."[158]

Lewis' harshest critic in this regard was Reinhold Niebuhr. In the light of his "supreme acquiescence," and particularly his acceptance of the Virgin Birth, Niebuhr accused Lewis of being a fundamentalist: ". . . Professor Lewis is a fundamentalist because he finds it necessary to nail down the 'revelation' which both fulfills and negates human culture with a 'fact' and therefore believes in the Virgin Birth. This is a pity."[159] Then Niebuhr immediately echoed the criticism that the others mentioned were also voicing:

Professor Lewis declares that science can have nothing to say about this fact because it is a matter of faith. In this he is surely wrong. Science cannot question the meaning which faith may assign to a fact. But if a structure of faith depends upon fact as fact it is in a sorry plight.[160]

Whether Niebuhr and the others' criticism of Lewis' understanding of the relationship between revelation and reason is valid, is, of course, open to debate. It is evident, however, that Niebuhr has misinterpreted Lewis' reason for accepting the Virgin Birth. According to Niebuhr, Lewis accepted it because he found it necessary to "nail down the revelation with a fact." However, the fact which Lewis used to "nail down the revelation" was not the Virgin Birth, as Niebuhr's statement seems to imply, but the Incarnation. Moreover, even if the "fact" which Niebuhr is referring to is the Incarnation, it still does not necessarily follow that because Lewis "nails down the revelation" with it, he therefore believes in the Virgin Birth. If that were the case, how could Brunner, who also "nails down the revelation" with the fact of the Incarnation, rejects the Virgin Birth as he does?[161]

Lewis' reason, then, for accepting the Virgin Birth, is not that which Niebuhr seems to imply. It is certainly not the reason behind the fundamentalists' acceptance of it,[162] and so it was wrong of Niebuhr to label Lewis as such. Instead, Lewis' rationale, as we have seen, was rooted in his conception of the Christian faith as an organic whole.

The Influence of Curtis

This leads us directly to what we have alluded to before,[163] viz., the influence of Lewis' teacher, Olin A. Curtis, upon his Christology and his theology as a whole.[164] During his earlier period, Lewis had moved away from Curtis, but from 1934 on he was in substantial agreement with him in many of his major emphases. It was, in fact, from Curtis that Lewis derived his understanding of the virgin birth as a part of a structural whole. Concerning it Curtis had stated:

. . . the virgin birth, nevertheless, belongs to the process of the Incarnation by the most

119

inherent fitness. To have the stupendous miracle of the Incarnation itself actualized by a natural method would be as much out of place as to have the sun rise without manifesting its nature in heat and light. The nature of the miracle should come out; the method should express the inner nature of the event.[165]

Curtis, following the lead of others such as H.L. Martensen,[166] thus made much of the structural wholeness of the Christian faith. As a systematic theologian it was his conviction that

Doctrines are all interlocked at the root. Between them there is an underlying philosophical connection. This philosophical connection must be revealed. Not only so, but the connection must be brought out in such a way as gradually to exhibit the Christian faith as one mighty organic whole.[167]

Lewis, with his philosophical cast of mind, was particularly amiable to this idea.

Curtis' influence is also evident in Lewis' understanding of the atonement. Although Curtis is careful to stress divine love, he roots his doctrine of the atonement in the holiness of God.[168] That God is holy means that he is absolutely perfect and absolutely moral.[169] Moreover since it is the "law of holiness" which brings all the attributes of God into harmonious reciprocity, holiness is "the finality, the fundament of all God's being."[170] The love of God thus becomes "the dynamic of the law of holiness."[171] It is the holiness of God "absolutely actualized in personal experience," and therefore "the most intensely moral feature in the whole life of the Godhead."[172]

The atonement, in turn, becomes the complete expression of the holiness of God: "Because God is holy he hates sin. Because he hates sin, the expression of that hatred is fundamental to any expression of God whatsoever. The death of Christ is the fundamental and exhaustive expression of God's hatred of sin."[173] However, that "exhaustive expression" is not an end in itself, but a means to an end: a new race of men and women in whom God's moral love is perfectly expressed.

Again, it is not difficult to discern the influence of Curtis on Lewis at this point. Like Curtis, Lewis makes divine holiness the starting point in his discussion of the atonement. Like Curtis, he sees the atonement as the highest expression of divine holiness and concurrently, the highest expression of divine love. Although he had rejected such a view and adopted a subjective theory of the atonement in his earlier Christology, now he returns, in the main, to the objective position of his former teacher.

Finally Curtis' influence is evident in Lewis' formulation of kenosis. Building upon the distinction between <u>schema</u> and <u>morphe</u> which he attributes to J.B. Lightfoot, Curtis explains what happened in the kenosis:

> As a preexisting person our Lord had two things, namely, first a divine nature with all the attributes of the Godhead; second, a divine personal experience equal to that of God the Father. The divine nature he did not give up, but has it eternally. But the divine experience he could and did give up in redemptional humiliation.[174]

Lewis, as we have seen, uses this same distinction and builds upon it in much the same way. In his earlier Christology he had rejected the kenotic theory because he believed it involved an impossible disruption in God's being and was incompatible with a progressive incarnation.[175] Now, however, he believes that this theory offers the best possible explanation of how the Word became flesh.

The Unique Features of Lewis'
Mature Christology

Yet there was a significant difference between Lewis and Curtis in their understanding of kenosis. According to Curtis, even while he was human, Jesus continued to possess every divine power and attribute. Against the charge that such a position destroys Christ's humanity, he argued that "it is possible for a person to have an attribute in the individual nature and yet not to have the attribute in self-consciousness."[176] A mother, for example, who by nature loves her child, can be asleep and thus unconscious of that love, yet still possess it nonetheless. As a human, then, Christ possessed all the divine attributes, but they were not always present in his consciousness.

Lewis, however, denied that the Incarnate Christ possessed divine attributes. He believed that any such possession, conscious or unconscious, destroyed Christ's humanity. Thus we are led to one of the unique features of Lewis' Christology. It is a Logos Christology, a Christology from above. Consequently he uses the kenotic theory to explain how the Eternal Word became flesh, and he establishes the continuity between the Eternal Word and the human Jesus by affirming the Virgin Birth. At one time Lewis had rejected both because he believed they confined the incarnation to one moment and as such denied the need for growth and development in the mind of Jesus. Now, however, he maintains both, but continues to insist on the very things that earlier he said they denied. Thus he maintains both a Logos Christology, a Christology from above, and a progressive incarnation, at least in part, a Christology from below! As Deane L. Shaffer notes, "His kenotic view of later years does not involve a relinquishing of the idea of process in the act of incarnation."[177]

As we have seen, Lewis develops this idea by describing, at times in great detail, the growing messianic concsiousness of Jesus. This had been a major concern in liberal Christology.[178] In fact entire volumes such as A.M. Garvie's <u>Studies in the Inner Life of Jesus</u> (1907) had been written in order to trace the process. Later, however, neo-orthodox theologians such as Brunner revolted against such efforts, considering them to be exercises in futility.[179] Lewis, on the hand, in his effort to maintain the full humanity of Christ goes to much greater lengths in attempting to describe the growing messianic consciousness of Jesus during the period when he formulated his mataure Christology than he ever had in his earlier more liberal days!

One can, of course, question the validity of such efforts, or the compatibility of the kenotic theory and the Virgin Birth with a progressive incarnation, but the efforts of Lewis do help to secure the essential humanity of Christ. In reference to Emil Brunner's classic, <u>The Mediator</u>, D.M. Baillie writes, "It is impossible to read his book without getting the impression that Brunner is not vitally interested in the life and personality of the Jesus of history, but only in the dogmas about him."[180] The same cannot be said of Edwin Lewis. His is no docetic Christology. Although he insists that we must begin with the Christ of faith, he is still very much interested in the Jesus of history. Thus, unlike some neo-orthodox theologians, Lewis is not guilty of over-reacting against the excesses of liberalism by emphasizing the divine Christ to the exclusion of the human.[181] Though one may raise questions concerning the internal consistency of his position, his Christ is fully human as well as fully divine.

The other unique feature of Lewis' mature Christology is his stress on the effect of the incarnation upon God. Lewis had first expressed this idea in "The Divine Triunity,"[182] written in 1918. There he had stated:

> The Incarnation therefore reaches into the very Godhead, affecting it profoundly, and was the supreme sacrifice that the Godhead was capable of making. There is in the Divine Personality an element that would not have been there had the Son of God not walked the earth as he did.[183]

It was not, however, until the period under consideration that he fully developed this idea.

Lewis had been led to this idea through his immersion in idealistic philosophy, and as has been previously shown,[184] particularly the philosophy of Andrew Seth Pringle-Pattison. Toward the conclusion of The Idea of God, for example, Pringle-Pattison states that "if we are to reach any credible theory of the relation of God and man, the traditional idea of God must be profoundly transformed."[185] He then goes on to describe that traditional idea as "a fusion of the primitive monarchial ideal with Aristotle's conception of the Eternal Thinker."[186] The result is a God who is abstractly perfect, but essentially self-centered and aloof from the world. Unfortunately, this idea has so influenced interpretations of the central Christian event, the incarnation, that its fundamental meaning has been obscured. According to Pringle-Pattison, the fundamental meaning is that of self-sacrifice, of losing one's life in order to find it. This, he says, is the conclusion he has been leading up to in his lectures:

No God, or Absolute, existing in solitary
bliss and perfection, but a God who lives in
the perpetual giving of himself, who shares
the life of his finite creatures, bearing in
and with them the whole burden of their
finitude, their sinful wanderings and
sorrows, and suffering without which they
cannot be made perfect.[187]

Lewis, then, under the influence of Pringle-
Pattison, developed his unique understanding of the
effect of the incarnation upon God.[188] We have already
discussed its main features,[189] but perhaps another
statement of Lewis' which captures its essence is in
order, and will bring our discussion of his mature
Christology to a fitting close:

Because of man's sin, something happened to
God's plan. Because of God's grace,
something happened to God himself. If one
dare write such words, God admitted into his
being an alien element, with the ensuing
necessity of undergoing structural
reorganization. The claim that there has
been such a structural change in God must be
true, and it must be a revelation, because
nobody could have had the audacity to imagine
it, and because the statement of it, with the
reasons that made the change necessary, has
such an overpowering influence on the mind
that accepts it. For evermore, the God of
the Christian bears a scar, and the scar is
not a birthmark he could not help but a wound
received in a freely chosen cause.[190]

1. See above, pp. 66-67.

2. Lewis, A Christian Manifesto, p. 13.

3. Cf. ibid., p. 221, and Edwin Lewis, A Philosophy of the Christian Revelation (New York: Harper and Row, 1940), p. 199.

4. Lewis, A Philosophy of the Christian Revelation, p. 179. See also Edwin Lewis, "The Question Concerning God," Theoolgy Today 1 (January 1945): 442.

5. Ibid.   6. Ibid., p. 200.

7. Lewis, A Christian Manifesto, p. 187. See also p. 191.

8. Ibid., p. 39.

9. Edwin Lewis, "The Doctrine of the Incarnation," class notes by David A. Seamands, 21 March 1944. Cf. Edwin Lewis, Christian Truth for Christian Living (Nashville: The Upper Room, 1942), pp. 14-15.

10. Edwin Lewis, "Revelation and Its Alternative," Religion in Life 11 (Spring 1942): 177.

11. Ibid., p. 181.

12. Edwin Lewis, "The Evangelical Experience and Faith," in Faith (Evanston: Garrett Biblical Institute, 1936), p. 88.

13. Edwin Lewis, "Evangelical," in The Ministry and the Sacraments, ed. Roderic Dunkerly (London: SCM Press, 1937), pp. 475-476.

14. Lewis, "The Doctrine of the Incarnation," 21 March 1944.

15. Edwin Lewis, The Faith We Declare (Nashville: Cokesbury Press, 1939), p. 216.

16. John A. Sims, "Revelation and Apologetic in the Theology of Edwin Lewis," p. 15. See also Deane

L. Shaffer, "The Theodicy of Edwin Lewis," p. 193.

17. Lewis, <u>A Philosophy of the Christian Revelation</u>, p. 98.

18. Ibid., p. 64. See also the chapter, "The Word As A Person," in <u>The Biblical Faith and Christian Freedom</u> (Philadelphia: Westminster Press, 1952), pp. 98-114.

19. Lewis, <u>The Biblical Faith and Christian Freedom</u>, p. 99.

20. Ibid.

21. Lewis, <u>A Philosophy of the Christian Revelation</u>, p. 96. See also p. 17.

22. See above, pp. 9-10.

23. Edwin Lewis, "The Humiliated and Exalted Son," <u>Interpretation</u> 1 (January 1947): 24. See also Lewis, <u>The Faith We Declare</u>, pp. 78-79.

24. Lewis, <u>A Philosophy of the Christian Revelation</u>, p. 96.

25. Ibid., p. 95.

26. Lewis, <u>The Biblical Faith and Christian Freedom</u>, p. 101.

27. Ibid., p. 100.

28. Lewis, <u>The Biblical Faith and Christian Freedom</u>, p. 60.

29. Lewis, <u>The Faith We Declare</u>, p. 39.

30. Lewis, <u>A Philosophy of the Christian Revelation</u>, p. 88.

31. Edwin Lewis, <u>A New Heaven and a New Earth</u> (New York: Abingdon-Cokesbury Press, 1941), p. 205. Cf. Lewis, <u>The Biblical Faith and Christian Freedom</u>, p. 98.

32. Lewis, "The Humiliated and Exalted Son," p. 24.

33. Lewis, _A Christian Manifesto_, p. 192.

34. Ibid., p. 188. See also Lewis, "The Question Concerning God," pp. 451-452.

35. Edwin Lewis, _Theology and Evangelism_ (Nashville: Tidings, 1952), p. 23.

36. Lewis, _The Biblical Faith and Christian Freedom_, p. 101.

37. Ibid., p. 109.   38. Ibid., p. 100.

39. Lewis, _A Philosophy of the Christian Revelation_, p. 175.

40. Sims, "Revelation and Apologetic in the Theology of Edwin Lewis," p. 25.

41. Lewis, _A Philosophy of the Christian Revelation_, p. 183.

42. Ibid., p. 48.   43. Ibid., p. 175.

44. Ibid., p. 98. See also, "The Question Concerning God," p. 449.

45. Ibid., p. 174.   46. Ibid., p. 202.

47. Ibid.   48. Ibid.

49. Ibid., pp. 180-189.

50. Ibid., p. 199. See also Lewis, "The Humiliated and Exalted Son," pp. 30-31.

51. Ibid., p. 184.   52. Ibid., p. 187.

53. Ibid., p. 189.   54. Ibid., p. 185.

55. Edwin Lewis, "The Christian Meaning of the Christmas Event," _The Christian Advocate_ 63 (23 December 1937): 1191-1192.

56. Edwin Lewis, "What the Resurrection Means to Me," _The Christian Advocate_ 70 (22 March 1945): 345.

57. Lewis, _A Philosophy of the Christian Revelation_, p. 202.

58. Ibid., p. 175. See also Lewis, "The Doctrine of the Incarnation," 2 February 1944: "God was held to be speaking and acting here as he had spoken and acted nowhere else; and to have spoken and acted in such wise that the result was finality -- it was never again needed."

59. Lewis, The Biblical Faith and Christian Freedom, p. 106.

60. Lewis, A Philosophy of the Christian Revelation, p. 90.

61. Ibid., p. 87.

62. Ibid., p. 85. Cf. Lewis, A New Heaven and a New Earth, p. 205.

63. Ibid., p. 50.

64. Edwin Lewis, "The Inevitable Theology of the Gospel Story," The Drew Gateway 17 (Summer 1946): 49.

65. Lewis, A Christian Manifesto, p. 98; See also, Lewis, The Faith We Declare, p. 68.

66. Lewis, "The Humiliated and Exalted Son," p. 30.

67. Lewis, The Biblical Faith and Christian Freedom, p. 104.

68. Ibid., p. 147. See also Lewis, The Faith We Declare, p. 52.

69. Lewis, A Christian Manifesto, p. 12.

70. Edwin Lewis, "The Man Christ Jesus," in Man (Evanston: Garrett Biblical Institute, 1938), p. 31.

71. Lewis, "The Inevitable Theology of the Gospel Story," p. 46. See also Lewis, A Philosophy of the Christian Revelation, pp. 53-54.

72. See especially Lewis, The Faith We Declare, p. 40, and Lewis, "The Humiliated and Exalted Son," pp. 20-32.

73. See above, pp. 25-27.

74. Lewis, "The Humiliated and Exalted Son," p. 25.

75. Lewis, A Philosophy of the Christian Revelation, p. 200. See also, The Biblical Faith and Christian Freedom, p. 113, where he states, "There is ontological continuity persisting through radical experiential change."

76. Lewis, A Christian Manifesto, p. 187. See also The Faith We Declare, p. 87, and "The Christian and His Creed," The Christian Advocate 68 (3 June 1943): 683.

77. Lewis, "The Humiliated and Exalted Son," p. 26.

78. Ibid., p. 27.

79. Lewis, "The Doctrine of the Incarnation," 16 March 1944.

80. Ibid., 20 April 1944.

81. Lewis, A Philosophy of the Christian Revelation, pp. 53-54.

82. Lewis, A New Heaven and a New Earth, pp. 129-144; "The Inevitable Theology of the Gospel Story," pp. 49-51; "The Resurrection of our Lord," in Sermons by the Sea (Nashville: The Abingdon Press, 1938), pp. 45-51. See also Lewis, "The Doctrine of the Incarnation," 2, 4, 9, 11 May 1944.

83. Lewis, A New Heaven and a New Earth, p. 135.

84. Lewis, "The Resurrection of our Lord," p. 45.

85. Lewis, A New Heaven and a New Earth, p. 136.

86. Lewis, "The Resurrection of our Lord," p. 45.

87. Ibid., p. 46.   88. Ibid., pp. 47-48.

89. Lewis, "The Inevitable Theology of the Gospel Story," p. 50.

90. Ibid., p. 51.

91. Lewis, A New Heaven and a New Earth, p. 140.

92. Lewis, "The Doctrine of the Incarnation," 27 January 1944.

93. Lewis, <u>A New Heaven and a New Earth</u>, p. 133.

94. Ibid., p. 134.

95. Lewis, "The Humiliated and Exalted Son," p. 26.

96. Lewis, "The Christian and His Creed," p. 683.

97. Lewis, <u>A Philosophy of the Christian Revelation</u>, p. 53.

98. Lewis, "The Humiliated and Exalted Son," p. 27.

99. Lewis, <u>The Faith We Declare</u>, pp. 91-92.

100. Lewis, <u>Jesus Christ and the Human Quest</u>, p. 295.

101. Lewis, <u>A Philosophy of the Christian Revelation</u>, p. 200. See also Edwin Lewis, "God Reconciling the World," <u>The Adult Bible Class Monthly</u> 27 (June 1934): 214.

102. Lewis, <u>A Christian Manifesto</u>, p. 191; cf. Lewis, <u>The Faith We Declare</u>, pp. 40-41.

103. Ibid.

104. Lewis, "The Christian and His Creed," p. 684.

105. Lewis, <u>A Philosophy of the Christian Revelation</u>, p. 200.

106. Lewis, "The Humiliated and Exalted Son," p. 29.

107. Lewis, <u>The Biblical Faith and Christian Freedom</u>, p. 112.

108. Lewis, "The Christian and His Creed," p. 684.

109. Lewis, <u>A Christian Manifesto</u>, p. 169.

110. Lewis, "The Humiliated and Exalted Son," p. 29.

111. Ibid., p. 22.

112. Lewis, <u>A Christian Manifesto</u>, p. 193.

113. Lewis, <u>The Biblical Faith and Christian Freedom</u>, p. 112.

114. Lewis, <u>A Christian Manifesto</u>, p. 179. See also Sims, "Revelation and Apologetic in the Theology of Edwin Lewis," p. 22.

115. Ibid.

116. Lewis, <u>A Philosophy of the Christian Revelation</u>, p. 200.

117. Lewis, "The Doctrine of the Incarnation," 14 March 1944.

118. Lewis, "The Humiliated and Exalted Son," p. 29.

119. Lewis, <u>The Biblical Faith and Christian Freedom</u>, pp. 112-113. See also Lewis, <u>A Philosophy of the Christian Revelation</u>, p. 201.

120. Lewis, <u>A Christian Manifesto</u>, p. 145.

121. Ibid., pp. 151-152.

122. Edwin Lewis, "The Evangelical Experience and Faith," in <u>Faith</u> (Evanston: Garrett Biblical Institute, 1936), p. 87.

123. Lewis, <u>A Christian Manifesto</u>, p. 146.

124. Lewis, "Lectures in Christian Theology," class notes by David A. Seamands, 4 January 1945. See also, Lewis, "The Evangelical Experience and Faith," p. 87.

125. Lewis, <u>A Christian Manifesto</u>, p. 147.

126. Ibid., p. 148.

127. Lewis, "Lectures in Christian Theology," 30 March 1944. Cf. Lewis, "The Evangelical Experience and Faith," p. 87.

128. Lewis, "The Evangelical Experience and Faith," p. 87. See also Lewis, <u>A Christian Manifesto</u>, p. 148.

129. Lewis, <u>Theology and Evangelism</u>, p. 54.

130. Lewis, <u>A Christian Manifesto</u>, p. 148.

131. Lewis, "The Evangelical Experience and Faith," p. 88.

132. Lewis, <u>A Christian Manifesto</u>, p. 149.

133. Ibid.

134. According to Lewis, the incarnation and the atonement are parts of the same whole, and there-fore cannot be separated: "Soteriology and Christology are the convex and the concave of the same arc" ("Recent Evidences of Theological Vitality," <u>The Drew Gateway</u> 16 (Winter 1945): 24). See also Lewis, <u>A Christian Manifesto</u>, p. 185.

135. Lewis, <u>A Christian Manifesto</u>, p. 161.

136. See above, pp. 151, 154.

137. Lewis, "The Humiliated and Exalted Son," p. 26.

138. Ibid., p. 27.   139. Ibid.

140. Edwin Lewis, "Salvation As Individual Experience," <u>Religion in Life</u> 121 (Autumn 1943): 537. See also Lewis, "The Inevitable Theology of the Gospel Story," p. 51.

141. Ibid. See also Lewis, "The Inevitable Theology of the Gospel Story," p. 51.

142. Edwin Lewis, "The Crucifixion," <u>Adult Bible Class Monthly</u> 31 (19 June 1938): 219.

143. Edwin Lewis, <u>The Ministry of the Holy Spirit</u> (Nashville: Tidings, 1944), p. 149.

144. Lewis, "The Inevitable Theology of the Gospel Story," p. 51.

145. Lewis, <u>The Biblical Faith and Christian Freedom</u>, pp. 143-144.

146. Ibid., p. 52. See also Lewis, "The Resurrection of Our Lord," p. 53; and <u>A Philosophy of the Christian Revelation</u>, p. 69.

147. Lewis, <u>A Christian Manifesto</u>, p. 162.

148. Lewis, "How Barth Has Influenced Me," p. 358.

149. Michalson, "The Edwin Lewis Myth," p. 219.

150. Lewis, <u>A Philosophy of the Christian Revelation</u>, p. 284.

151. Emil Brunner, <u>The Mediator</u>, trans. Olive Wyon (Philadelphia: Westminster Press, 1947), p. 232. See also Chapter 7, "The Divine Word," pp. 201-231.

152. Ibid., p. 316. Cf. Lewis, <u>A Philosophy of the Christian Revelation</u>, p. 200.

153. Ibid., pp. 156-157.   154. Ibid., p. 162.

155. Ibid., p. 169.

156. J.S. Bixler, Review of <u>A Philosophy of the Christian Revelation</u>, by Edwin Lewis, in <u>Christendom</u> 6 (Spring 1941): 265.

157. George W. Davis, Review of <u>A Philosophy of the Christian Revelation</u>, by Edwin Lewis, in <u>The Crozer Quarterly</u> 18 (July 1941): 269.

158. Edward T. Ramsdell, Review of <u>A Philosophy of the Christian Revelation</u>, by Edwin Lewis, in <u>The Journal of Religion</u> 21 (July 1941): 323.

159. Reinhold Niebuhr, Review of <u>A Philosophy of the Christian Revelation</u>, by Edwin Lewis, in <u>New York Herald Tribune Books</u>, 17 November 1940, p. 30.

160. Ibid.

161. Brunner, <u>The Mediator</u>, pp. 322-327.

162. Lewis is critical of J. Gresham Machen's <u>The Virgin Birth of Christ</u> because he defends the doctrine in typical fundamentalist fashion: on the basis of the documentary evidence. See Lewis, <u>A Philosophy of the Christian Revelation</u>, pp. 187-188.

163. See above, pp. 32-33.

164. For Lewis' moving tribute to his former teacher, see Edwin Lewis, "The Rev. Olin Alfred Curtis," in The Teachers of Drew, pp. 108-112. Also see his acknowledgement in "The Course of Contemporary Theological Thinking: An Examination of a Prediction Made Twenty-five Years Ago by Professor Curtis," Drew Gateway 7 (April 1936): 1-2. Curtis' prediction can be found in "A New Estimate of the Theological Situation," The Methodist Review Quarterly 37 (October 1911): 627-640.

165. Curtis, The Christian Faith, p. 234.

166. Lewis, A Philosophy of the Christian Revelation, p. 332.

167. Curtis, The Christian Faith, p. 183.

168. Ibid., p. 257.   169. Ibid., p. 263.

170. Ibid., p. 264.   171. Ibid., p. 265.

172. Ibid.   173. Ibid., p. 328.

174. Ibid., p. 241.

175. See above, pp. 25-27.

176. Curtis, The Christian Faith, p. 244.

177. Shaffer, "The Theodicy of Edwin Lewis," p. 182.

178. See Lawton, Conflict in Christology, pp. 165-188.

179. Brunner, The Mediator, pp. 358-359.

180. Donald M. Baillie, God Was in Christ (New York: Charles Scribners Sons, 1948), p. 35.

181. For a description of this over-reaction, see ibid., pp. 34-39.

182. See above, pp. 2-3.

183. Lewis, "The Divine Triunity," pp. 290-291.

184. See above, pp. 12-21.

185. Pringle-Pattison, The Idea of God, p. 407.

186. Ibid.   187. Ibid., p. 411.

188. Lewis thus stands with the growing number of Christian theologians in the late 19th and 20th centuries who have challenged the orthodox conception of divine impassibility. It is significant that J.K. Mozley cites the work of Pringle-Pattison as contributing to that shift (The Impassibilty of God, (London: Cambridge University Press, 1926), pp. 136-7). For a recent discussion of this trend in theology see Warren McWilliams' The Passion of God: Divine Suffering in Contemporary Protestant Theology (Macon Georgia: Mercer University Press, 1985).

189. See above, pp. 161-165.

190. Lewis, A Christian Manifesto, pp. 169-170.

Chapter 4

FROM MONISM TO DUALISM

In the foreward to <u>The Creator and the Adversary</u>
published in 1948, Lewis announced that he was setting
forth a position which was "in sharp contrast at a
crucial point"[1] to anything he had previously written.
In the past, he explained, he had found it easy to
accept a monistic point of view. However following his
shift "from philosophy to revelation," as he had
continued to reflect upon the meaning of revelation, he
found himself gradually led to a dualistic position.
Although there were scriptures which seemed to root the
complexities of existence in a single source, this was
not the overall thrust of the revelation. Instead the
scriptures, taken as a whole, portray a God of holy
love who has an Adversary whit whose opposition he must
continually reckon. This opposition is in very much
more than the will of man. It goes down to "the very
roots of existence."[2]

Such a view, Lewis maintained, clearly demanded "a
philosophy of conflict, whose elements are fundamental
and irreconcilable opposites."[3] It was such a
philosophy which he sought to present in his book, a
philosophy which, he had come to believe, meant a frank
abandonment of traditional monism which would have us
ultimately root evil in the will and purpose of God.
Although such a position had generally been held
sacrosanct, Lewis nevertheless insisted, "There is
nothing sacred about monism, and to question it is not
blasphemy, especially while the memory of the recent
universal holocaust still haunts our very dreams.
Perhaps the blasphemy is with monism!"[4]

Later we will return to <u>The Creator and the
Adversary</u> to examine the dualistic position which Lewis
offers as an alternative to monism. But it is
important to recognize that, as in the case of <u>A
Christian Manifesto</u> which marked the climax of his
transition "from philosophy to revelation," <u>The Creator
and the Adversary</u> marked the climax of the transition
to dualism,[5] and as such represents the end result of a
gradual shift that had been taking place in Lewis' mind
for several years. David Soper is thus correct in his
assessment that the movement toward dualism "had
already begun in the mind of Lewis before <u>The Creator</u>

and the Adversary."[6]   Thus before discussing the
dualistic position he formulates there, it will be
instructive for us to trace that movement as closely as
possible.[7]

Intimations in the "Manifesto"

The first intimations of such a movement can be
detected in the work which, we have just noted, marked
the climax of Lewis' earlier transition, viz., A
Christian Manifesto.   There we observe two elements in
the discussion which indicate that already another
movement in Lewis' thought was commencing.

First, Lewis portrayed the conflict between good
and evil much more vividly than ever before:

> The figure of the horrific Apollyon in
> Pilgrim's Progress represents more than
> imagination: it represents dire reality. It
> is not for nothing that men have felt a
> malignant spirit hovers over them and at any
> moment might crash down upon them.[8] Nobody
> but a facile optimist can face the spectacle
> of this twentieth-century world and not feel
> that a malign spirit is at work.   The
> Zoroastrian visualized the world as the arena
> for the death grapple of the Spirit of Light
> and the Spirit of Darkness. Always has it
> seemed to men of the East that a wild beast
> "couched at the door," awaiting its moment to
> spring. The Hebrew felt it and he passed on
> his feeling as a heritage to Christianity.[9]

Lewis therefore chided the modern church, with its
sentimental theism, for underestimating the magnitude
of the conflict.   "Then is it not high time that we
awaked out of sleep?   We are in the midst of a Titanic
struggle: it is the struggle between the demonic and
the divine."[10]   He also pinpointed the cause of the
modern church's failure: "We have become so monistic,
which unfortunately means all too often naturalistic,
and will have nothing to do with the thought of some
great reality that is opposing the will of God, and
that may even oppose it effectively."[11] Lewis made it
clear that he was not advocating a return to the
ancient cosmogony of Satan and his angels, but admitted
that if he was forced to choose, he would rather have
the church recommitted to that cosmogony for it
"to accept an easy-going evolutionary naturalism and

settle down passively and innocuously to the chanting of the pious sentiment, 'God's in his heaven, but all's well with the world.'"[12]

In stressing the reality of the demonic element, Lewis described it as "a necessary feature of created existence."[13] Yet he was careful to point out that this did not imply a Zoroastrian dualism where evil is eternal. Instead, "The evil of the world comes into existence, like space and time, with the world itself: there is evil only as there is creation. This conclusion would seem to be demanded by the doctrine of the sovereignty of God."[14] Later Lewis would modify his position and posit the existence of evil prior to creation. At this point, however, in keeping with the traditional orthodox understanding of divine sovereignty, evil was still viewed as part of the permissive will of God.

The other element in the Manifesto which signified a step in the direction of dualism was Lewis' surrender of the concept of divine omniscience. In the past, he stated, he had adopted a metaphysical view of God which took omniscience for granted, or at least made it inevitable.[15] But as he had contemplated the grace of God as revealed in the redemption of humanity, the growing sense that he must choose between omniscience and grace "created a dilemma which only those can fully appreciate who have gone through a similar experience."[16]

According to Lewis, omniscience implies that the redemptive act of God in Christ stemmed from divine necessity, not from divine grace. Prior to the creation of men and women God knew that they would fall into sin, and that the death of his son would therefore be necessary for their redemption. Such was the view of his teacher, Olin Curtis, who had taught that "the postulate of the whole plan of salvation was the divine omniscience."[17]

Lewis, however, believed that such a view, although it made room for grace by making it the motive of creation, actually destroys the ultimate meaning of grace because it implies that God had no choice in the matter since in creating men and women he was obligating himself to redeem them. In his concern, then, to emphasize the freedom of God's gracious activity, Lewis proposes "the divine adequacy"[18] rather than the divine omniscience as the postulate of the

139

whole plan of redemption.

According to his scheme, "God in the very creation of man as a being of alternative possibilities sets limits to his knowledge."[19] He is thus like a creative artist who discovers and expresses his inherent possibilities as each situation arises; he is not like a builder mechanically working from a pre-existing blueprint. Lewis even presents Christ's growing realization that he must die to redeem humanity as a possible symbol of what was going on in the Divine Mind itself.[20] In summarizing his position he states:

> In a word, as between a grace that is the postulate of creation because it is supposed that the Creator is omniscient without any qualification, and a grace that is a consequence of creation because the Creator meets an unexpected and tragic situation -- as between these two conceptions of grace, the second is the one that seems most fully to agree with our Christian faith, in particular with the claim that in Jesus Christ God of his grace made atonement for the sin of the world."[21]

Revelation in Terms of Conflict

In 1940, Lewis published[22] what his successor Carl Michalson considered his most significant work,[23] A Philosophy of the Christian Revelation. Here in a chapter entitled "The Spirit of Anti-Christ,"[24] Lewis again paints the reality of evil in bold strokes. "The simple truth is that implicit in the fact of Christ is the fact of Anti-Christ."[25]

Still he was unwilling to attribute metaphysical reality to evil, viewing it instead in Augustinian fashion as the privation of good. "Anti-Christ is not a being, not even a metaphysical entity, except in so far as the principle of negation may be so described."[26] As a result, although he did not question the propriety of the scripture in dramatizing the conflict by portraying evil in personal, superhuman terms, he believed that ultimately it could be accounted for in terms of human freedom and without reference to a superhuman force.

However, it was the last chapter of the book, entitled "The Drama of Man's Deliverance,"[27] which was most indicative of the shift which was occurring in Lewis. Having established a philosophy of the Christian revelation, he now proposes the method of presenting the revelation which, he believes, will afford its greatest acceptance. This method involves presenting Christian truths imaginatively, not scientifically; it means appealing primarliy to the emotional, not the rational nature of humans. According to Lewis this is a method consistent with the scriptures, particularly the New Testament, where repeatedly the work of Christ is described in metaphorical language.[28] It is also in keeping with this method that he advocates a dualistic interpretation of the revelation:

> It is a question whether there is still any better and any truer way to express the content of the Christian revelation than the way which might be called dualistic. Dualism supposes opposites and it supposes conflicts, and where there are opposites and conflicts there is always the possibility of defeat or victory. And if there is anything of which the ordinary man is most keenly aware, it is just this fact of opposites and conflicts. He might be a theoretical monist, but he never talks monistically when he is talking about the deepest aspects of his experience. One might say that the language of dualism is man's natural language, and it is his natural language because it agrees so exactly with what is forced upon his attention every day, both within his life and without it.[29]

Lewis, however, insists that he is not advocating a metaphysical dualism. Rather he wishes to "recognize a 'cosmological dualism.'"[30] Thus although dualism is a necessary result of the creative process, prior to creation there is only one.[31]

Lewis went on to argue that only such a dualistic interpretation was consonant with the facts of everyday experience, the larger movements of society and history, and the meaning of scripture. He then concluded the chapter by presenting, for the first time, an interpretation of the work of Christ from the standpoint of dualism.

Conflict in Heaven

In January 1941, Lewis delivered the Quillian Lectures at Emory University. These lectures were amplified and published the next year under the title, _A New Heaven and a New Earth_. In relation to his movement toward dualism, this work is significant in that for the first time Lewis argued that evil could not be accounted for solely in human terms but was ultimately rooted in a superhuman source. This was in keeping with his central thesis that one's view of "heaven" determines one's view of "earth."[32] The reason, then, that there is war on earth is because there is already war in heaven. The conflict which is at the roots of human existence (earth) thus is a reflection and extension of the conflict in the realm of divine existence (heaven). The figure of Satan, in turn, stands for the "more-than-human phases of the moral struggle, and therefore for a metaphysical phase."[33]

Lewis finds support for his view in the apocalyptic literature of later Judaism which appropriately portrays the conflict between the divine and the demonic in dramatic terms. But in keeping with the view of apocalypticism, and in contrast to the absolute dualism of Zoroastrianism, he again stresses

> The evil is not an eternal fact, and it is not a direct creation. Instead, the evil is the good gone wrong. Actually, therefore, God created one, but the one became two. It became two by division. The evil acquired a quasi-independence, but it never can become wholly independent.[34]

Lewis can therefore still affirm the traditional understanding of the sovereignty of God. "And what God has created, God can use, God can control, God can destroy."[35]

Evil and the Christian Life

The next step in Lewis' movement towards dualism occurred in his two books on Christian living which were published in 1942. Actually in one of these, _The Practice of the Christian Life_, he did not advance beyond his Quillian lectures, but simply reiterated what he had said concerning both the super-human character of evil and the sovereignty of God.[36]

However, in the other, <u>Christian Truth for Christian Living</u>, Lewis suggested for the first time that evil may have been in existence even before creation:

> We ordinarily suppose that when God undertook creation, he faced a perfectly open field. There was nothing for him to consider except what he purposed to do. But we may be wrong in our supposition. It may be that God found that the field was not open. It may be that the very first step he took toward creation revealed to him the fact that the field was not open. It may be that the very first step he took toward creation revealed to him the fact that he must expect to meet opposition throughout the whole long process he had now initiated. Quite possibly God knew this <u>before</u> he began; but if he did not, then as he began to carry out his purpose he became aware of an enemy.[37]

Lewis realized that many would hesitate in accepting this proposal, but perhaps, he explained, such was necessary for God himself -- in order for Him to fully express his nature.

> Perhaps there are some things which even God can get only as he "pushes against" something else. Perhaps there is a form of creativity which even God can exercise only where there is opposition. Or if the statement seems a little too extreme, let us modify it, and say that something that is alien to God's essential nature provides the very opportunity whereby all that is in God's nature -- his holiness, his love, his sacrificial grace -- may manifest itself. It is just because, as was said above, the field is <u>not</u> open, that God can undertake to possess as he does.[38]

Some might still reject such a proposal on the grounds that it denies God's power and self-sufficiency, but they are still left with the problem of accounting for evil. And the more they accentuate divine power and self-sufficiency, the more they complicate that problem for themselves.[39]

The Impact of World War II

The following year, 1943, there appeared in the
<u>Drew Gateway</u> Lewis' article "The War and Theology." An
intense, hard-hitting essay provoked by the grim
realities of World War II, in relation to Lewis'
transition from monism to dualism, it parallels his
"Re-Thinking Missions" and "Fatal Apostasy" articles in
terms of their relation to his earlier transition. In
the light of the War, Lewis attacked theological
liberalism for its naive optimism:

> It is a sad commentary on the smug
> complacency of our much vaunted "modernity"
> that it has taken a world revolution to bring
> it to the judgment bar of Scripture.
> Standing at the bar, it hears the merciless
> sentence: "Thou are weighed in the balance,
> and found wanting."
> In its chastened mood, theology is
> likely to abandon the illusion of inevitable
> and necessary progress. The fact that stands
> up sheer and stark today is that the evil may
> destroy the good.
> So optimistic was liberal theology . .
> . The first World War administered something
> of a shock to the general complacency . . .
> but the shock proved not to be fatal . . . To
> an extent one hardly likes to admit, the
> whole educational procedure of the Western
> world, alike in church and state, has been
> based on this optimistic idea of inevitable
> progress. And he who sows the wind is likely
> to reap the whirlwind.[40]

Lewis maintained that behind the idea of
inevitable progress there lay a philosophy -- one which
inevitably took some form of monism. It was this
philosophy which was ultimately to blame for the situation. Yet in the light of world events, monism, like
the idea of progress implied within it, was also
weighed and found wanting.

> But he is a brave man, or more certainly, a
> man of myopic vision, who can regard the
> spectacle of a world falling apart, and still
> affirm, "All is One!" If there is one thing
> that all things can never be for the
> understanding man of today, it is <u>one</u> <u>thing</u>!
> The very least he will be satisfied with is

144

-- two things. And not two things one of
which must "inevitably" prevail, but two
things so evenly matched that the outcome is
always in doubt -- except to faith. Two
things utterly different from each other! . .
. And not two simply in the sense of one and
one, but two in the sense of the completely
and absolutely and irreconcilably
antithetical.[41]

Until this time, Lewis had been unwilling to posit
a metaphysical dualism. Although he had presented the
conflict between good and evil as inherent in the
nature of existence, he had always maintained that
behind the duality there was an underlying unity. Now,
however, he was willing to take another step towards
that position: he denied that such a unity exists.

If we are told that there is an a priori
metaphysical necessity of unity to which we
must pay respect, the answer will have to be
that any alleged metaphysical a priori which
patently requires a man to be a liar, and
declare that things are not what they are, is
purely imaginary. Let such an a priori be
dressed up in the most imposing vocabulary
that even a Hegel could devise, and we shall
refuse to be convinced. "Still, whatever
happens, I will not lie!" -- not even as the
price of admission to the Ancient Order of
Monistic Metaphysicians. No! Our task is
not to postulate a metaphysical unum and then
proceed to refund back into it all the
diversities of experience, until these
diversities disappear because everything is
now seen to be the same as everything else.
That may be very good Spinozism, and very
good Hegelianism, and very good Haeckelism,
but it is not Biblicism and it is not
Christianity and it is not "the testimony of
experience."[42]

When we consider the scriptures, what do we find? Not
an "assemblage of easy-going, all accomodating
monisms,"[43] but conflict written on every page. From
the very start, beginning with the serpent in the
Garden, the battle lines are drawn. It is a battle
which "makes Zoroastrianism so alluring, and all
pantheistic monisms of whatever stripes so
incredible."[44]

145

Lewis admitted that his reflections, provoked by a world at war, had not been set down systematically and therefore might lack logical coherency; yet he insisted that they were indicative of the direction in which future theology should move. His own theology, of course, did continue to move in that direction, but in relation to that movement, "The War and Theology," is significant because it signaled his decisive break with monism. Having thus said "farewell" he was now free to embrace dualism and to begin developing his own particular dualistic metaphysic.

Lectures in Christian Theology

Notes of Lewis' classroom lectures in Christian theology taken by David A. Seamands in 1944, and H. Bufkin Oliver in 1946, along with Marvin Green's doctoral dissertation[45] provide us with our next significant source in tracing the development of Lewis' dualism.

In his 1944 lectures, for example, Lewis again presents the idea he had first advanced in Christian Truth for Christian Living that God himself needs the opposition of evil in order to fully express his nature. He does this by raising a number of rhetorical questions:

1.   Is the frustration of God's original purpose by evil and sin a necessary condition of God's own complete self-discovery?

2.   Is God unaware of the range and depth of the resources of his own suffering love except as a situation arises that calls them forth?

6.   Could God have known all the truth about himself if he had been content to remain forever a solitary being -- remote and detached and solitary?[46]

Lewis acknowledges that from the standpoint of traditional Christian metaphysics, even to raise such questions is anathema. But he asks, "Are not these suggestions prompted by the Bible, and is not this the metaphysic demanded by the Biblical Revelation?"[47]

Later Lewis also hinted at what that metaphysic might be. In doing so he describes that other form of reality which exists over against the Creative Reality, God. "The other form may not be creative at all: it may rather be a power of recalcitrance, a capacity to hinder the creative, an inherent opposition with which the Creative Reality has always to reckon."[48] As such this other form of reality has no power of its own: it is purely negative, and thus requires the presence of the positive before it can go into effect. "It can do nothing of itself; it only gets in the way. It cannot create life; it can only put limits on life."[49] So Lewis concludes, "it may be in some such fashion we find the solution to our most baffling problem."[50]

However Lewis does not explicitly state in his 1944 lectures that this other form of reality is absolute or eternal; thus there is no categorical affirmation of metaphysical dualism. Consequently, Marvin Green, in summarizing Lewis' position in 1945 can still say, "While this evil has no metaphysical reality; inasmuch as it is not eternal, it is no less a force opposing God."[51]

But in his 1946 lectures this is no longer the case. Evil has clearly become a metaphysical reality -- passive, yes -- but "nothing less than absolute."[52] When therefore God decides to create, he "cannot wholly determine the conditions of creation." Creation is more than an expression of his will. "It has a plus and the plus is of evil."[53]

In venturing a metaphysic to account for this fact, Lewis proceeds to outline the same essential position that is found in The Creator and the Adversary which was published two years later. Of course, his argument there is much more detailed and comprehensive, but its main lines can be found in these lectures including the distinction between existence and existents,[54] and the delineation of the three forms of existence -- divine, demonic, and residue.[55] At times, in fact, there is an almost word for word correspondence between his 1946 lectures and his 1948 book.[56] Since we will soon be examining the position Lewis sets forth in the book, we will not discuss it here; but it is clear that two years before its publication, by 1946, all the main features of Lewis' dualistic metaphysic had been worked out. By that year, then, the transition from monism to dualism had been completed.

Lewis' Norton Foundation Lectures

In March 1947, Lewis delivered the Norton Foundation Lectures at Southern Baptist Theological Seminary. Three of these lectures later appeared in The Review of and Expositor.[57] Because of his topic, "Philosophy and the Fourth Gospel," a full exposition of his dualistic metaphysic was inappropriate. However it is not difficult to detect that metaphysic behind many of his statements. For example, Lewis insisted, as he had on previous occasions, that to best speak to the contemporary situation a philosophy of existence must be expressed in terms of conflict. That was why he had chosen to expound the fourth gospel; there one finds a philosophy of the Christian revelation couched in those very terms. Thus through his use of metaphors such as light and darkness, life and death, flesh and spirit, etc., the author of the fourth gospel is expressing his understanding of the conflict which underlies all existence. When the divine exercises creativity, a principle of opposition, a "factor of hostility" is revealed. It "relative to this condition that the Word creates."[58] The present world is therefore an arena where a conflict between contending forces is being waged. Life is a battlefield, not a playground; and although the "ultimate metaphysic" of the conflict is "open to discussion," no one can question the fact of the conflict itself.[59]

In his lectures, then, Lewis was not explicit about the metaphysic of his dualism, but it was implicit throughout. Later these lectures were incorporated into one of the chapters of The Creator and the Adversary.[60]

The Creator and the Adversary

In 1948, with the appearance of The Creator and the Adversary Lewis' metaphysical dualism was finally made explicit to all. Here he argues that the glaring reality of evil in everyday experience forces us to conceive of it not as a mere negation of the good, but as a positive metaphysical reality. Moreover this understanding of evil is confirmed by the Christian revelation contained in the scriptures. Hence both experience and revelation would have us account for the fact of evil not, as has traditionally been done, by positing a metaphysical monism, but by positing a metaphysical dualism.

In developing his own particular dualistic metaphysic, Lewis argues that the traditional conception of God as Pure Being is too abstract to account for the biblical God who is personally involved with creation. The biblical picture is that of "a God who was deeply and sacrificially <u>interested</u> <u>in</u> <u>a</u> <u>cause</u>, and consequently a God who was aware of opposition and preparing to meet it."[61] To account for this opposition Lewis thus offers his metaphysic, recognizing that it is "no more than 'a speculative venture' and is to be considered as such."[62] According to that metaphysic, there can be <u>existents</u> only as there is a prior <u>existence</u>. In the beginning, then, there is not God, but existence. Existence, however, is "under a necessary law of self-differentiation,"[63] and thus gives rise to three primal existents: the creative divine, the discreative demonic, and the neutral residue. But there is no chronological order in their appearance; each existent is equally eternal and each is always limited by the other two. Lewis offers no explanation as to why existence differentiates itself in this particular fashion, but simply states, "It is that way because it is that way."[64]

He then describes each of the existents. The residue or "residual constant" provides the "substance of whatever is created" and never increases or decreases in its total quantity.[65] It functions much like Aristotle's "potentiality" or Plato's "non-being." It cannot create, but provides a necessary condition for creation. In sum it is "the permanent possibility of empiric actualities."[66] Only through the residue can Form, which originates in the creative divine, be actualized into particular forms.

In characterizing the creative divine, Lewis notes that in light of the concept of the <u>imago dei</u>, "we have the advantage of an analogy with ourselves."[67] Thus we can speak of God as living, personal, rational and good because we observe these qualities in humans whenever they are involved in the creative process. Of course, the Christian faith requires us to go beyond simply describing the divine nature in terms of human analogies. It requires us to see God as a complex being, and to see his complexity as the ground of his creative and redemptive activities. It is this complexity which "prevents God from being an impersonal Solitary, and makes him instead a socially complete Person."[68] Moreover, this complexity can be explained by the operation of the same law of necessary self-differentiation which caused primal existence to give rise to three primal existents. "It is by virtue of this law that God is, in the language of Christian tradition, a Trinity."[69] In accordance with this, there is no chronological sequence intended when we describe God as Father, Son, and Holy Spirit -- only an order of necessary relationships.

The third eternal existent, the discreative demonic, is best conceived as the supreme antitype of the creative divine. "It is the purely irrational, the purely immoral, the purely malign, the purely destructive. Its nature is such that it can tolerate nothing but itself."[70] To speak of the demonic merely as a principle does not go far enough; to speak of it as a person goes too far, since it lacks rational and moral qualities. "'He' clearly says too much; 'it' seems to say too little."[71] It is best, then, to think of the demonic in semi-personal terms.

Moreover, if in the analogy of a perfectly good man we get out best clue to the nature of the divine, so in a perfectly bad man -- degenerate, disorganized, dehumanized -- we get our best clue to the nature of the demonic. "A completely bad man would be discreative corruptibility become absolute."[72] However, unlike a completely bad man, the demonic cannot initiate anything, but only has the power to hinder or obstruct the creative activity of the divine.

This, then, is Lewis' dualistic metaphysic of existence upon which he bases his understanding of creation and redemption. Thus God knows that if he creates he will encounter the opposition of the Adversary. But he accepts this "necessity" and in doing so allows the Adversary to lay a burden of suffering both upon himself and his creation. The creative act is therefore not pure joy for God, but "a song which is also a cry."[73] Thus when God spoke the creative Word, the conflict began; and the conflict continues wherever He is active causing him "continual frustration."[74]

Lewis, then, accepts the concept of a limited God. God is free in his purpose to create, but limited in respect to the conditions in which he creates. Moreover, God is also limited by time which Lewis holds is ontologically real. It is within a temporal framework that the conflict is set, and the outcome "contains always an element of contingency -- and God must reckon with this contingency."[75] This, in turn, implies a real limitation in God's foreknowledge and power, although Lewis insists that they are sufficient to enable him to accomplish his purpose.

It also implies a revised conception of divine sovereignty. Since God must operate under conditions for which he is not solely responsible, it is best to describe it as the sovereignty of a father, not that of an oriental despot.[76] It is therefore a sovereignty of love, not power; a sovereignty which is adequate, but not absolute.

In humanity, the conflict between the Creator and the Adversary reaches its highest magnitude. Because of the impact of the demonic upon them, humans become alienated from God and thus fail to realize his purpose for them. God therefore sends his Son who enters into mortal combat with the Adversary. On the cross, the decisive battlefield, God proves himself the stronger. He has more to give than the Adversary;[77] his giving grows out of his holy love. When humans receive that love through faith, they enter into eternal life against which death and destruction cannot prevail. Although mortal combat with the Adversary continues, victory has been assured for all who have received that life.

We will, of course, be examining Lewis' conception of the work of Christ in more detail, but this, in brief, is the position which Lewis set forth in The Creator and the Adversary. It is, however, important to stress what is already evident: Although Lewis' dualism is real, it is not absolute. In an absolute dualism, the two opposing forces are equal and the conflict is never finally resolved. For Lewis, however, such is not the case. As Deane Shaffer observes, "the two opposing forms of primal existence -- God and the Adversary -- are not in necessary balance."[78] God is greater than the Adversary: "He can outsuffer him; he can outventure him; he can outplan him. For he can love and he can love even unto death, and the Adversary, whose weapons are vanity and frustration and corruption and sin and death, cannot do that."[79] Thus there is never any serious doubt as to the final outcome of the conflict. His dualism, is therefore a modified dualism, and as such allows for hope. As David Soper notes, "Lewis' dualism is not as absolute as it seems; he is after all, a Christian

151

first, and a dualist second; he insists upon the reality of hope."[80] Grounded then in the death and resurection of Christ, the believer is assured that the Adversary will ultimately be subjected to the Creator's purpose.

The Response to Lewis' Dualism

In complete contrast to A Christian Manifesto, the climax of Lewis' earlier transition which evoked such a widespread and intense response, The Creator and the Adversary which climaxed his transition to dualism evoked very little. Perhaps theologians and pastors had learned to expect the unexpected from Edwin Lewis! Of course, reviews of the book did appear in a number of theological journals, and it continued to be discussed by later critics and interpreters of Lewis.

The majority expressed appreciation for his position at several points. For one, they applauded his willingness to face the fact of evil with such utter seriousness. Appearing as it did in the aftermath of World War II and the holocaust when many were confronted with the grim reality of evil as never before, Lewis' position struck a responsive chord because it gave evil the full recognition that those events seemed to demand. As Howard Kuist wrote in Religion in Life, "In view of the intense accentuation of the strife between good and evil forces in our present world, this issue of a malignant Adversary cannot be shrugged off."[81] Every serious person, he insisted, "must reckon with this brilliant interpretation of the Christian faith."[82]

Later interpreters of Lewis were also appreciative of his position at this point. Charley Hardwick, who is generally critical of Lewis' theology, nevertheless praised him for sensing a need for a better accounting of evil, and called his attempt "an admirable goal."[83] David Soper, in contrasting Lewis' conception of evil with Nels Ferre's,[84] also expressed appreciation for the realism of Lewis:

> Sentimentality, however disguised, seems to be, and is, peering over Ferre's shoulder. Lewis' view has at least no softness; it is no siren song. It does not make the monistic mistake of modifying the distinction between good and evil; it does not underestimate the reality and tragedy of evil.[85]

Another aspect of Lewis' position which was commended by many was his willingness to avoid any _a priori_ commitment to the metaphysical concept of God which has dominated the Christian tradition. Lewis is adventuresome enough to be willing to consider an alternative to classical Christian monism in the face of aspects of experience which raise doubts about such a monism. Edgar Sheffield Brightman, of whom Lewis had often been critical for his rooting of evil within the being of God, thus applauded Lewis for his "growing mind" and his "courageous originality" in going beyond traditional Christian theism.[86]

According to Soper, Lewis was willing to stand "against the stream" because his primary concern was not to produce a tidy metaphysical system, but to accentuate the reality of the moral conflict. Thus even though we may not be able to accept Lewis' "split infinity," we "cannot fail to stand up and cheer Lewis' ethical seriousness."[87] Like Reinhold Niebuhr, Lewis believed it was "better for religion to forego perfect metaphysical consistency for the sake of moral potency."[88] In thus choosing an adequate ethic over an adequate metaphysic, Lewis had chosen the better part.

These, then, were what others perceived as the major strengths in Lewis' position. However, they were also quick to point out areas where they felt it was problematic.

Edgar Sheffield Brightman, for example, wondered "how on the divine-demonic-residue basis, can he account for a regular, law-abiding system of nature?"[89] If, as Lewis had maintained, the conflict was truly cosmic in nature, it would drastically effect the natural order as well as the human. However scientific evidence overwhelmingly indicates a fundamental regularity and uniformity in the natural world. Even events such as earthquakes and volcanic eruptions, though often cited as evidence to the contrary, actually illustrate the fundamental order of nature since they too are the result of well-understood geological processes. As such they argue for a universe, not a multiverse as Lewis' position implies.

Paul Schilling's objection is similar: "It is by no means clear that, as Edwin Lewis maintains, the concept of the demonic is 'as indispensable as the concept of the divine.'"[90] Echoing Augustine, he insists that in our experience good does have a positive ultimate quality which evil lacks. Whereas good can stand on its own, "evil is derivative, meaningless apart from its contrast with good."[91]

Thus both Brightman and Schilling question whether Lewis' position adequately accounts for the facts of experience. Others on the other hand, questioned whether he had adequately interpreted the Christian revelation. Paul Minear, for example, while acknowledging the dualistic thread running through the biblical witness, maintained that the biblical dualism was "more carefully limited"[92] than Lewis'. One need not therefore be so willing to surrender God's sovereignty, his power to create ex nihilo, or his power to reconcile all creation to himself. Likewise Frederic Greeves felt that Lewis had failed to grasp "the peculiar tension of the Hebrew-Christian faith which finds room for Good and Evil within a Theism that does not qualify the statement: 'In the beginning God.'"[93]

David Soper also raised objections at this point. In rejecting creation ex nihilo and therefore the divine origin of the discreative and the noncreative, he believed Lewis had gone too far. "No one will deny their existence, and few will deny that their 'meaning' is given them by God, but many will justly question whether their 'existence' is self-explanatory."[94] Likewise Deane Shaffer maintained that by making existence rather than God primary, Lewis had introduced an idea that was foreign to the biblical witness. As a result, he could only base his argument on the silence of scripture.[95]

Charley Hardwick's critique of Lewis' interpretation of the revelation was even more penetrating. He questioned whether Lewis' fundamentally speculative approach to the problem of evil was not antithetical to the approach of the Bible. Although it may be an interesting response to the problem of evil, the biblical response is "not metaphysical but geschichtliche eschatological."[96] Once Lewis is allowed to raise the question in metaphysical terms, he has already decided the case. "The problem is whether the conceptuality which makes it necessary to raise the question is not itself inadequate to the Bible."[97] Frederic Greeves voiced the same objection when he stated that Lewis seems to be unable to appreciate the uniqueness of the Hebrew religion in its treatment of dualism "as a fact but never as a solution."[98]

Finally, there were those who pointed out an apparent inconsistency in Lewis' position. If good and evil are both ultimate, as he maintained, what reason is there to believe that good will eventually triumph? Kenneth J. Foreman thus suggested there is a lack of harmony between Lewis' metaphysics and his religious faith:

> As a metaphysician he says that God and the Adversary can never destroy each other; evil inheres in the framework of existence, which God creates eternally; yet on the other hand (speaking religiously) he looks forward to the ultimate triumph of the Creative God. How can this be? . . . If God from the beginning is faced with a neutral constant and a demonic Adversary, where is any guarantee that these will not continue to thwart him to the end?[99]

Paul Minear raised the same objection. Like Zoroastrianism, he argues, Lewis' position never really answers the question of how "a primal dualism can ever eventuate in a final monism."[100] Moreover, if one can affirm such a monism at the end, why not also affirm it at the beginning?

Such, then, were the major criticisms leveled against Lewis' dualism. We will return to one of these in our discussion of the central problem in Lewis' theology. Now, however, we turn to consider the effect of his dualism on his Christology.

1. Edwin · Lewis, <u>The Creator and the Adversary</u> (New York: Abingdon-Cokesbury Press, 1948), p. 7.

2. Ibid.   3. Ibid.

4. Ibid.

5. It is interesting to note a further similarity between the two works. The earlier was a "manifesto," the later Lewis described as "a <u>confessio fidei</u>" (ibid., p. 9). As such both were kept free from the ordinary paraphernalia of scholarship (notes, references, etc.) since Lewis wanted nothing to obscure his own position.

6. Soper, <u>Major Voices in American Theology</u>, p. 31.

7. Deane L. Shaffer has briefly traced the transition in his study, "The Theodicy of Edwin Lewis," pp. 259ff.

8. Lewis, <u>A Christian Manifesto</u>, p. 153.

9. Ibid., pp. 207-208.   10. Ibid., p. 210.

11. Ibid., p. 208.   12. Ibid., p. 209.

13. Ibid., p. 210.   14. Ibid., pp. 210-211.

15. Ibid., p. 158.   16. Ibid.

17. Ibid., p. 156.   18. Ibid.

19. Ibid., p. 158.   20. Ibid., pp. 158-159.

21. Ibid., p. 159.

22. Actually the manuscript was completed in the Spring of 1939, but publication was delayed for about a year. See Lewis, <u>A Philosophy of the Christian Revelation</u>, pp. xi-xii.

23. Michalson, "The Edwin Lewis Myth," p. 218.

24. Lewis, <u>A Philosophy of the Christian Revelation</u>, pp. 12-131.

25. Ibid., p. 123.   26. Ibid., p. 125.

27. Ibid., pp. 288-306.   28. Ibid., p. 294.

29. Ibid., p. 295.   30. Ibid., p. 341.

31. Ibid.

32. Lewis, A New Heaven and a New Earth, pp. 5-6.

33. Ibid., pp. 98-99.   34. Ibid., p. 94.

35. Ibid.

36. Edwin Lewis, The Practice of the Christian Life
     (Philadelphia: Westminster Press, 1942), pp. 93-
     104.

37. Lewis, Christian Truth for Christian Living, p.
     127.

38. Ibid., p. 128.   39. Ibid., p. 129.

40. Edwin Lewis, "The War and Theology," The Drew
     Gateway 14 (Winter 1943): 13-14.

41. Ibid., p. 14.   42. Ibid.

43. Ibid.   44. Ibid.

45. Marvin W. Green, "Contemporary Theories of Evil.
     An   Ethical   View: Reinhold   Niebuhr;   A
     Philosophical View: E.S.   Brightman;   A
     Theological View: Edwin Lewis." Green worked
     under Lewis' supervision and was allowed to use
     Lewis' own lecture notes in preparing his thesis
     (Personal   interview with Marvin W.   Green,
     Madison, New Jersey, May 17, 1980).

46. Edwin Lewis, "Lectures in Christian Theology,"
     class notes by David A. Seamands, 2 May 1944.

47. Ibid.

48. Edwin Lewis, "Lectures in Christian Theology," p.
     250, quoted in Green, Contemporary Theories of
     Evil, II, p. 363. See also Lewis, "Lectures in
     Christian Theology," class notes by David A.
     Seamands, 2 May 1944.

49. Lewis, "Lectures in Christian Theology," class notes by David A. Seamands, 2 May 1944.

50. Ibid.

51. Green, "Contemporary Theories of Evil," II, p. 428.

52. Edwin Lewis, "Lectures in Christian Theology," class notes by H. Bufkin Oliver, 24 January 1946.

53. Ibid., 12 February 1946.

54. Ibid., 14 March 1946.

55. Ibid., 19, 26 March 1946.

56. Cf. the summary of Lewis' position found in his lectures (ibid., 23 April 1946) with essentially the same summary in The Creator and the Adversary, pp. 176-177.

57. Edwin Lewis, "Philosophy and the Fourth Gospel: The Philosophic Mind," Review and Expositor 44 (July 1947): 271-284; "Philosophy and the Fourth Gospel: The Word Became Flesh," 44 (October 1947): 430-443; "Philosophy and the Fourth Gospel: The Timeliness of the Timeless," 45 (January 1948): 18-34.

58. Lewis, "Philosophy and the Fourth Gospel: The Word Became Flesh," p. 439.

59. Lewis, "Philosophy and the Fourth Gospel: The Timeliness of the Timeless," p. 19.

60. Lewis, The Creator and the Adversary, pp. 181-194.

61. Ibid., p. 141.

62. Ibid., p. 140.

63. Ibid., p. 141.

64. Ibid.

65. Ibid., p. 143.

66. Ibid.

67. Ibid., p. 144.

68. Ibid.

69. Ibid.

70. Ibid., p. 145.

71. Ibid., p. 146.

72. Ibid.

73. Ibid., p. 138.   74. Ibid., p. 127.

75. Ibid., p. 164.   76. Ibid., p. 148.

77. Ibid., p. 127.

78. Shaffer, "The Theodicy of Edwin Lewis," p. 272.

79. Lewis, The Creator and the Adversary, p. 26.

80. Soper, Major Voices in American Theology, p. 34.

81. Howard Tillman Kuist, Review of The Creator and
    the Adversary by Edwin Lewis, in Religion in Life
    18 (Winter 1948-1949): 148.

82. Ibid.

83. Charley Hardwick, "Edwin Lewis: Introductory and
    Critical Remarks," p. 100.

84. Ferre's interpretation which accentuated divine
    sovereignty appeared one year before Lewis'. See
    Nels F.S. Ferre, Evil and the Christian Faith
    (New York: Harper and Bros., 1947).

85. Soper, Major Voices in American Theology, p. 35.

86. Edgar Sheffield Brightman, "A Growing Mind," The
    Drew Gateway 20 (Winter 1950): 3.

87. Soper, Major Voices in American Theology, p. 35.

88. Reinhold Niebuhr, Does Civilization Need
    Religion?, p. 214, quoted in ibid., p. 35.

89. Brightman, "A Growing Mind," p. 4.

90. S. Paul Schilling, God and Human Anguish
    (Nashville: Abingdon, 1977), p. 106.

91. Ibid.

92. Paul S. Minear, Review of The Creator and the
    Adversary by Edwin Lewis, in Theology Today 6
    (April 1949): 142.

93. Frederic Greeves, Review of The Creator and the
    Adversary by Edwin Lewis, in The London Quarterly
    and Holborn Review 174 (October 1949): 363.

94. Soper, <u>Major Voices in American Theology</u>, p. 35.

95. Shaffer, "The Theodicy of Edwin Lewis," p. 338.

96. Hardwick, "Edwin Lewis: Introductory and Critical Remarks," p. 101.

97. Ibid.

98. Greeves, Review of <u>The Creator and the Adversary</u>, p. 363.

99. Kenneth J. Foreman, Review of <u>The Creator and the Adversary</u> by Edwin Lewis, in <u>Interpretation</u> 3 (January 1949): 109.

100. Minear, Review of <u>The Creator and the Adversary</u>, p. 143.

Chapter 5

THE TRIUMPHANT CHRIST

Christology in Terms of Conflict

Lewis' transition from monism to dualism had a noticeable effect upon his Christology. However in contrast to his earlier transition, the effect in this case was not nearly as profound or far-reaching. Thus his conception of the person of Christ remained substantially the same. Christ is still the Eternal Word who appeared in human form in the person of Jesus of Nazareth. In presenting the Christology which resulted from his dualism we will therefore not discuss Lewis' conception of the person of Christ since we would only be repeating what has already been outlined above.[1] Rather we will concern ourselves exclusively with that aspect of his Christology where his transition to dualism had its major effect, viz., his conception of the work of Christ.

Having chosen to interpret the revelation in terms of a philosophy of conflict, Lewis now views the work of Christ from that standpoint. The Christ-event thus becomes the focal point of the conflict between the Creator and the Adversary:

> The history of Jesus Christ, from the Annunciation to the Ascension, is a dramatic representation of the conflict which lies at the very heart of existence, and of the principles and processes by which alone the conflict can issue in divine and human triumph.[2]

"Christ was the Creator's supreme achievement in the struggle with the Adversary."[3] In fact, Lewis insists that only when it is conceived in this way does "the drama of the Man Christ Jesus" have its "full significance."[4]

God Fully Enters the Conflict

The incarnation therefore signifies God's "personal participation" in the conflict, his entering into the struggle with the Adversary "to the uttermost possible extent that his own nature permits."[5] In his previous efforts to reveal himself to humankind, God had encountered the opposition of the Adversary, but did not feel its full force until he assumed the human form:

> Elsewhere, the Word works upon the darkness, so to speak from the outside. But now the Word comes directly, personally, into the sphere of the darkness, and he comes in that form which the darkness can most completely frustrate. He comes in the form of the human.[6]

The "darkness," i.e. the Adversary, can "most completely frustrate" the human form because it is the highest expression of God's creative activity and therefore provides the Adversary with the greatest opportunity for discreative activity. If then God is to win the victory over the Adversary, it must be won here:

> It is in the human, therefore, where the most is at stake, and where the battle goes the hardest, that God himself is most involved and must make his supreme effort. But his supreme effort is also his most costly effort. It is an effort calling for the Creator to clothe himself in that human flesh whose essential mortality makes it certain that the Creative Will will know not only the numerous ills to which flesh is heir, but will know the impact of shattering death. <u>God becomes man to save men by his conquest over the Adversary</u>.[7]

By assuming human flesh God, in the person of his Son, thus "insinuates himself into the very center of the arena of the conflict,"[8] and thereby exposes himself to the severest onslaughts of the enemy.

The various episodes of the incarnate life such as Christ's birth, development, temptation, suffering, death and resurrection, thus suggest "how real and how dire even for God the Creator is the conflict which is inseparable from created existence."[9] Throughout his incarnate life the Son of God stood unflinchingly against the power of the Adversary. He recognized the evil so prevalent in humanity, but refused to allow it a place in his own heart. Through his acts of healing he fought against pain and disease "regarding them as abnormalities -- something having no intrinsic right in God's universe, something indicative of a still deeper disturbance, and something therefore which must be eradicated."[10] He spoke on occasion of a veritable kingdom of evil which was opposed to the kingdom he had come to establish. He knew that more was needed than the means whereby men and women could be reconciled to God: the very destruction of evil had to be guaranteed. "There is an enemy alike of God and man -- and that enemy is why he was here. He came to give himself as a ransom, He would come to a death-grapple with the elemental evil -- slay it as mythic heroes slew the great dragon."[11] Yet Christ did not fight the enemy with his own weapons. At every point he met the self-assertiveness of the Adversary with self-forgetfulness; he answered hate with love.

This then is the achievement of the incarnation. Christ was tried and tempted as every human is, he felt the full force of the demonic as every human feels it, yet he never succumbed to its power. "To live the life of the Spirit in the conditions of the flesh, beset with the impact of evil, knowing continually the assaults of the Adversary -- this is what the Son of God did; this, indeed, is the very meaning of the Incarnation."[12]

The Final Battle

Yet to insure the ultimate defeat of the Adversary, one final battle had to be fought and won. To live in the conditions of human flesh was not enough. He must experience the enemy's cruelest blow: death. For death "always means that the destructuve (discreative) principle has prevailed."[13] And when it prevails over the highest form of God's creative activity, where his very image has been stamped, it represents the ultimate expression of the Adversary's power. If then he would break that power, he must enter the realm of death.

The cross is therefore the final battleground, the place where the Creator and the Adversary meet in one final grapple:

> Calvary was the meeting-place of the elemental powers of existence -- and if anyone wants to say the Hosts of Heaven and the Hosts of Hell, he has New Testament warrant for doing so. The daring language

represents _metaphysical_ _reality_. Jesus is no
longer as the Good Samaritan, dealing with
results. He would deal with the cause. He
was now as the apocalyptic Rider on the White
Horse, his eyes like a flame of fire, his
garment sprinkled with blood, behind him the
armies of heaven. He was looking for the
Beast. Only when the Beast itself was
chained, would the days of the brood of the
Beast be numbered. He met the Beast in the
Beast's own den -- and the Beast came out
licking its chops, leering its horrid
triumph . . . Incarnate Love met Incarnate
Hate, and when the sound and fury of that
decisive clash had ceased, all that was left
to mortal sight was a Cross against the sky,
and on it a broken form, mute evidence of the
defeat of Love.[14]

But what appeared to be the final defeat of Love
was, in fact, the final defeat of Evil. The Adversary
inflicted his cruelest blow upon the Son of God not
realizing that in doing so he had thereby inflicted a
death blow to himself. This is what the early church
fathers, with their strange metaphor of the hook and
the bait, were trying to convey. Often that mataphor
has been ridiculed; seldom has its profound meaning
been grasped. It was

. . . a way of saying that when the Son of
God, "the Word became flesh," entered the
realm of the Adversary, came under the
Adversary's power, and received the blow of
the Adversary's last weapon, which is death,
and was securely bound in the tomb behind the
great stone which effectively barred the door
-- that when that happened it was not the Son
of God who suffered defeat, but the
Adversary.[15]

The Divine Triumph

That the Son of God did in fact win the victory is
established by the Resurrection. Christ emerged from
the tomb as victor over death. He bound it and opened
the gates of eternal life. The resurrection is
therefore "the evidence of God's domination."[16] It
reveals that there is a power greater than death -- the
power of creative love:

164

The Resurrection is the dramatizing of the finality and indestructibility of self-giving love. It is a way of saying, in one overwhelmng and inescapable divine word, that victory belongs to the cause with which Jesus Christ is forever identified . . . For all time and to all men the word has been spoken -- that the triumph of Christ is the promise of universal triumph.[17]

The resurrection thus guarantees that evil does not have the last word, that human life has ultimate meaning, that evil does have a limit, and that there is life beyond death and destruction -- eternal life. Through faith men and women can enter into and possess that life now; and although they continue to experience the opposition of the Adversary, they are certain of the ultimate triumph of God.[18]

Such then is the conception of the work of Christ which resulted from Lewis' transition to dualism. Essentially is is a restatement of what Gustaf Aulen calls "the dramatic view"[19] of the work of Christ which was common among the early church fathers, and which had been revived by Aulen in his provocative study, Christus Victor, published in 1931. Lewis, of course, was well-acquainted with Aulen's study[20] but his adoption of the dramatic view should not be directly attributed to Aulen's influence. Rather he found in Aulen's study confirmation of the direction in which he himself, as a result of other factors, was already moving.

Before turning to discuss those factors, however, we would point out that during the course of his career Lewis, at different times, advocated each of the three main theories of the atonement.[21] In his early theology, when his primary concern was the human quest, he was mainly interested in how the work of Christ affected humanity; thus a moral influence theory of the atonement. Later when the focus of his theology was the divine self-disclosure, he was concerned with how the work of Christ affected God; therefore a satisfaction theory. And finally, when he was occupied with the problem of evil, he presented the work of Christ in terms of a triumph over the demonic; hence a ransom or classical theory of the atonement.

Reasons for the Transition to Dualism

Unfortunately Lewis never wrote an article as he did following his earlier transition where he himself tried to account for his shift from monism to dualism. Yet in the preface of <u>The Creator and the Adversary</u> he does briefly touch upon this issue. There he claims that the shift to dualism was a logical consequence of his earlier shift which had led him to take the revelation seriously:

> While here and there in the Scriptures the complexities of existence appear to be traced to a single source, this is not the meaning of the completed self-disclosure. Its meaning, rather, is that the God of holy love has an Adversary with whose opposition he must continually reckon . . . This actuality must be a Christian postulate: revelation demands it, and experience at every point supports it.[22]

Based then on statements such as this, both Deane Shaffer[23] and John Sims[24] maintain that it was Lewis' concern to take the revelation seriously that ultimately caused the transition. Shaffer, for example, states, "it was the shift to Scripture as the chief influence on his thought that finally did lead to a shift from monism to dualism. The more he considered the totality of the self-revelation of God, the more convinced he became that monism ignored the facts of the revelation."[25]

There is, of course, little doubt that this was one of the major reasons for Lewis' shift to dualism. However, to present Lewis' concern to take the revelation seriously as the sole or even the primary reason for the transition fails to probe deep enough. After all, many other theologians during this period were endeavoring to take the revelation seriously -- just as seriously as Edwin Lewis -- yet very few were led to a metaphysical dualism as a result. Although they took evil and human sinfulness much more seriously than the earlier optimistic liberals, the vast majority still adhered to a metaphysical monism. They were not inevitably driven, as Lewis was, to a dualistic position.

Additional reasons must therefore be advanced to fully account for Lewis' transition. Mention should be made of external events such as World War II and the holocaust. We have already observed the effect of the War on Lewis,[26] as well as his statement in <u>The Creator and the Adversary</u> that to question monism is not blasphemy "especially while the memory of the recent universal holocaust still haunts our very dreams."[27] These crisis events forced Lewis and other theologians to come to grips with the reality of evil as never before. Thus there was a renewed interest in the problem of theodicy and books such as Ferre's which dealt with this problem appeared during this time.

Mention should also be made of the influence of other theologians on Lewis, and in this regard, particulary Nicholas Berdyaev.[28] Deane Shaffer suggests that in relation to the problem of evil Berdyaev was "the one man in contemporary theology that seemed to challenge his thinking."[29] He notes Lewis' summary of Berdyaev's position in <u>A Philosophy of the Christian Revelation</u>,[30] and also observes the similarity between Berdyaev's concept of primary irrational freedom and Lewis' concept of primal existence.[31] Berdyaev's influence, however, was much like Barth's in relation to the earlier transition -- more provocative than persuasive. It was not his particular metaphysical structure which appealed to Lewis; he found that "more curious than convincing."[32] What did appeal to him was Berdyaev's frank recognition of evil and his willingness to try to account for it.[33] In that Lewis found encouragement to continue in the direction in which he was already going.

Finally, and we would maintain, the decisive reason for Lewis' shift from monism to dualism can be attributed to certain philosophical presuppositions concerning the nature of God which he derived from Andrew Seth Pringle-Pattison. As we noted earlier[34] Pringle-Pattison advocated a profound transformation in the traditional idea of God. That traditional idea, which he described as the idea of "a God without a universe, a pre-existent, self-centered, and absolutely self-sufficient Being eternally realizing a bliss ineffable in the contemplation of his own perfection,"[35] was based upon an abstract conception of divine perfection where God is "a changeless and self-sufficient unit."[36] He therefore proposed an alternate conception where "the movement to the finite and the realization of the infinite in the finite"[37] determined the nature of divine perfection. Thus instead of defining God in terms of "the perpetual undimmed enjoyment of a static perfection . . . We must interpret the divine on the analogy of what we feel to be profoundest in our own experience."[38]

It was his fundamental agreement with Pringle-Pattison at this point, viz., his insistence upon defining divine perfection in terms of human perfection which ultimately paved the way for Lewis' dualism. Thus he redefines divine omnipotence, omniscience, and sovereignty all in terms of human analogies. He insists that to be meaningful God's love and concern for humanity must be viewed within a temporal framework. He advocates a conception of a limited God believing it is preferable to the abstract impersonal conception of traditional Christian theism. David Soper criticized Lewis' metaphysical dualism because "it makes God no more and no less than an enormously large man -- proportionally no better equipped than man to overcome evil."[39] Such, however, was in keeping with Lewis' understanding of divine perfection.

Given then Lewis' concern to present the revelation in terms of conflict, and his acceptance of Pringle-Pattison's understanding of divine perfection, we can see why he was able to posit dualism, not merely as a fact, but as a solution. In traditional Christian theism, such a dualism means that God ceases to be God. However, Lewis' God, conceived of in Pringle-Pattison's terms, can function within a dualistic framework.

NOTES TO CHAPTER 5

1. See above, pp. 95-110.

2. Lewis, <u>A Philosophy of the Christian Revelation</u>, p. 305.

3. Lewis, <u>The Creator and the Adversary</u>, p. 259.

4. Lewis, <u>A Philosophy of the Christian Revelation</u>, p. xi.

5. Edwin Lewis, "The Creative Conflict," <u>Religion in Life</u> 21 (Summer 1952): 399. See also Edwin Lewis, "Is God Really Omniscient?," <u>Religion in Life</u> 20 (Spring 1951): 186.

6. Lewis, "Philosophy and the Fourth Gospel: The Word Became Flesh," p. 443.

7. Lewis, <u>The Creator and the Adversary</u>, p. 154.

8. Lewis, "Philosophy and the Fourth Gospel: The Word Became Flesh," p. 440.

9. Lewis, <u>The Creator and the Adversary</u>, p. 153. See also Lewis, "Lectures in Christian Theology," class notes by H. Bufkin Oliver, 12 February 1946.

10. Lewis, <u>A Philosophy of the Christian Revelation</u>, p. 301.

11. Ibid., p. 302.

12. Lewis, <u>The Creator and the Adversary</u>, p. 193.

13. Lewis, "The Creative Conflict," p. 399.

14. Lewis, <u>A Philosophy of the Christian Revelation</u>, pp. 302-303.

15. Lewis, <u>The Creator and the Adversary</u>, pp. 155-156.

16. Lewis, <u>A Philosophy of the Christian Revelation</u>, p. 303.

17. Ibid. See also Lewis, <u>The Creator and the Adversary</u>, p. 156.

18. Lewis, <u>The Creator and the Adversary</u>, p. 177.

19. Gustaf Aulen, <u>Christus Victor; An Historical Study of the Three Main Types of the Idea of Atonement</u>, trans. A.G. Hebert (New York: Macmillan Co., 1931).

20. See Lewis' concise summary of Aulen's argument in <u>A Philosophy of the Christian Revelation</u>, pp. 297-299.

21. Although, as we have already suggested, there was overlapping in his later theology when he adhered to a form of both the satisfaction theory and the ransom or classical theory. See above, p. 116.

22. Lewis, <u>The Creator and the Adversary</u>, p. 8.

23. Shaffer, "The Theodicy of Edwin Lewis," p. 34.

24. Sims, "Revelation and Apologetic in the Theology of Edwin Lewis," p. 51.

25. Shaffer, "The Theodicy of Edwin Lewis," p. 34.

26. See above, pp. 143-146.

27. Lewis, <u>The Creator and the Adversary</u>, p. 8. See above, p. 192.

28. See especially Nicholas Berdyaev, <u>Freedom and the Spirit</u>, trans. Oliver Fielding (London: Centenary Press, [1935]); <u>The Divine and the Human</u>, trans. R.M. French (London: Robert MacLehouse and Co., 1945); <u>The Destiny of Man</u>, trans. Natalie Duddington (London: Robert MacLehouse and Co., [1937]).

29. Shaffer, "The Theodicy of Edwin Lewis," p. 292.

30. Lewis, <u>A Philosophy of the Christian Revelation</u>, pp. 279-282.

31. Shaffer, "The Theodicy of Edwin Lewis," pp. 305-308.

32. Lewis, <u>A Philosophy of the Christian Revelation</u>, p. 280.

33. Ibid., p. 296.

34. See above, pp. 123-124.

35. Pringle-Pattison, _The Idea of God_, p. 399.

36. Ibid., p. 340.   37. Ibid.

38. Ibid., p. 411.

39. Soper, _Major Voices in American Theology_, p. 32.

CONCLUSION

The Fundamental Problem of
Lewis' Theology

The influence of Pringle-Pattison in relation to Lewis' dualism brings us to what we would maintain is the fundamental problem in Lewis' theology. Jameson Jones describes it well:

> The problem of Lewis comes in his refusal ever to separate completely his biblical faith and philosophical structure. His concern with reason, metaphysics, philosophical problems reflects a continuing in the liberal tradition. He spoke of making a reasonable case for the revelation, and thus betrayed his own position.[1]

This problem is bound up with what was always for Lewis the central task of theology, the task he was engaged in throughout his career: the integration of revelation and philosophy, of the Christian faith and existence as a whole.

In his early theology he approached this task from the standpoint of a philosophy arrived at apart from the Christian revelation, and then sought to ground the Christian revelation in that philosophy. Later, however, he came to the conclusion that one could not approach the task in that manner without mutilating the revelation at many crucial points. So he moved "from philosophy to revelation," and in doing so, changed his approach to the task by making the Christian revelation, not a particular philosophy arrived at apart from it, his starting point.

The task, however, remained the same. Although he had changed his approach, he never questioned the validity of the task itself, nor prescribed the limits to which it could be carried out. As he put it, "In a word, the fact of faith and the fact of revelation do not dispense with rational reflection. It is still necessary to relate faith and revelation to the whole movement of existence."[2]

Lewis believed that this task could be carried out because the Christian revelation with which he now began contained within itself its own philosophy:

173

> . . . it throws a light that reaches the
> outermost bounds of thought. Passed through
> the alembic of the mind, it leads to its own
> metaphysic, it moves straight to its own
> deductions, and it discovers in all the
> complexities and apparent discords of
> existence that perfect round of meaning in
> which its finality is attested.[3]

He was convinced, then, that it was possible to derive
a philosophy from the Christian revelation, "to round
it out into a <u>Weltanschauung</u>."[4]

It was, however, his failure to recognize the
limitations of such an endeavor which constitutes the
fundamental problem of Lewis' theology. For although
Lewis is correct in maintaining that the fact of
revelation does not dispense with rational reflection
and the need for philosophical structure, there is a
point at which all efforts to rationalize the
revelation break down. The finite mind is simply
unable to fully comprehend the self-disclosure of the
infinite; human categories are inadequate to explain
divine revelation. Thus although the attempt to
formulate a philosophy of the Christian revelation is a
worthy and necessary endeavor, it can only be carried
out in an incomplete manner, one which never will
afford the human mind complete intellectual
satisfaction.

In certain instances the Christian revelation
presents us with evidence which our rational categories
cannot assimilate. In those instances we must either
deny the evidence or revise our categories. When we
cannot deny the evidence or see how our categories can
be revised, we are at a point where it is best to
suspend judgment, in other words, acknowledge mystery.

Lewis, however, in his concern to formulate a
philosophy of the Christian revelation, is at times
unwilling to suspend judgment when he should. His
insistence upon working out in philosophical categories
what he perceived as the dualism of the Christian
revelation is a case in point. Although he admits it
is only a "speculative venture," would it not have been
wiser in this case to have suspended judgment, to have
recognized the fact of dualism in the revelation
without making it a solution?

As Charley Hardwick suggests, such a speculative

venture is contrary to the intent of the revelation:

> Lewis' approach to the problem of evil is fundamentally speculative. Confronted with the reality of evil, his aim is to account for it within the general structures of reality . . . Nevertheless, it is well established that the approach of cosmological speculation is not, in the first instance, relevant to the intent of the Biblical writings. In the case of the Fall, for instance, as implicit as certain metaphysical views may be in the story, the basic intent and meaning is missed if these views are expanded. This means that the Christian response to evil is quite different from a metaphysical account of its status in reality.[5]

By insisting, then, on such a venture Lewis actually ends up distorting the meaning of the revelation which he is so concerned to clarify. But is this not always the case when attempts to expound the revelation in rational, philosophical categories go beyond the bounds of their inherent limitations?

The Promise of Lewis' Theology

Yet bound up with this fundamental problem is also what we would maintain is the promise of Lewis' theology. Some, of course, see little or no promise in his theology. In an article written less than five years after Lewis' death, Charley Hardwick noted "the curious and even ironic fact" that in such a short time Lewis' work was being "almost totally ignored."[6] He maintained however, that there were valid theological reasons for this, particularly Lewis' supernaturalism which Hardwick argued was irrevelant to the theological needs of modern man:

> His argument that he can make a supernaturalist position meaningful to modern man by showing him that the nature of reality cannot be exhausted on naturalistic grounds does not really carry any persuasive power except to those who come to his thought already convinced of his position.[7]

Hardwick thus concluded his largely critical assessment of Lewis' theology by quoting Reinhold Niebuhr's caustic remark that Lewis was a fundamentalist.[8]

That Lewis' work seemed to hold little promise to neo-liberals like Hardwick, and even many neo-orthodox theologians is easy to understand. Like Albert Knudson they believed that in his revolt against naturalistic liberalism he had gone too far, and was trying to revive a theology "that many regard as outmoded."[9] Thus they could never come to terms with his supernaturalism, his acceptance of a literal resurrection and virgin birth, or his understanding of the relationship between faith and historical science. Although Lewis was not a fundamentalist, at certain critical points he simply came too close to that position to be taken seriously by many in the mainstream of American theology. This is what Halford Luccock meant when he attributed the rapid passing of Lewis' theological influence to his "getting off the Methodist symbol." Consequently, "it became hard to distinguish his Neo-Orthodoxy from his Fundamentalism."[10]

Conservatives, on the other hand, while accepting the very parts of his theology which liberals rejected, also had problems with Lewis. They could never come to terms with Lewis' acceptance of biblical criticism,[11] his metaphysical dualism,[12] and his pre-occupation with rational and philosophical questions. Thus although they tended to find more promise in Lewis' theology than liberals, they too rejected it at certain critical points.

But perhaps the promise of Edwin Lewis' theology does not lie as much in its material content as in the way in which, given his own individuality and his historical context, he approached the theological task itself. Very early in his career he wrote,

> One thing no man can do for long is to violate the peculiar structural law of his own individuality. A person constituted as John Henry Newman was will never come to peace until he can rest back upon "authority." On the other hand, persons constituted like Huxley or Tyndell or Spencer will be satisfied only with personal and independent judgments, and so they succeed in reaching these, they want nothing more.[13]

What then was the peculiar law of Lewis' individuality?

It can best be described by a phrase from Wordsworth's "Ode to Immortality" which Lewis used as the title for one of his Norton Foundation lectures: "the philosophic mind."[14] Thus for Lewis, implicit in the task of theology was the "search for a comprehensive standpoint," one that would "make our whole picture of existence intelligible."[15]

In his case, however, not violating his own individuality was a costly matter. It means adopting positions which were decidedly against the theological currents of his day; it meant being misunderstood and harshly criticized by others. Yet Lewis, in being true to himself, was willing to accept the consequences rather than sacrifice his own theological integrity. In his review of The Creator and the Adversary, Edgar Sheffield Brightman stated,

> At no time has Edwin Lewis' mind been guided by any other consideration other than a search for vital Christian truth. Because of this motivation he turned a few years ago from liberalism to a more conservative view. It is this same motivation that now leads him to a new emphasis.[16]

Herein lies the problem of Edwin Lewis. The content of his theology, though constructive, will probably remain forgotten. But in his struggle to maintain his own theological and intellectual integrity regardless of the personal cost and consequences, he remains a permanent model for all who undertake the task of theology.

NOTES TO CONCLUSION

1. S. Jameson Jones, "Three Representative Leaders in Contemporary American Methodist Theology," p. 303.

2. Lewis, "Philosophy and the Fourth Gospel: The Philosophic Mind," p. 276.

3. Lewis, "The Question Concerning God," p. 443.

4. Lewis, "How Barth Has Influenced Me," p. 358.

5. Charley Hardwick, "Edwin Lewis: Introductory and Critical Remarks," pp. 100-101.

6. Ibid., p. 91.   7. Ibid., pp. 101-102.

8. Ibid., p. 103. For Niebuhr's comment see above, p. 180.

9. Albert C. Knudson, Review of A New Heaven and a New Earth by Edwin Lewis, Religion in Life 10 (Autumn 1941): 623.

10. William J. McCutcheon, "The Theology of the Methodist Episcopal Church During the Inter-War Period," p. 371.

11. Harold John Ockenga, "A Christian Manifesto: Anti-Modernist But Unorthodox; A Critique," Christian Faith and Life 41 (July 1935): 226-231.

12. Deane Shaffer, "The Theodicy of Edwin Lewis," p. 338.

13. Edwin Lewis, "Two Antithetical Types: Abelard and Bernard of Clairvaux," Methodist Review 98 (January 1915): 54.

14. Lewis, "Philosophy and the Fourth Gospel: The Philosophic Mind," pp. 271-284.

15. Ibid., pp. 275-276.

16. Edgar Sheffield Brightman, "A Growing Mind," p. 3.

INDEX

A

Ahlstrom, Sydney, 79
Anthropology, 12ff.
Appolinarius, 104
Aquinas, 104
Atonement, 18ff, 31, 111ff,
    119, 165ff
Aulen, Gustaf, 165

B

Baille, D.M., 122
Barth, Karl, 68ff, 75,
    76, 79ff, 117, 167
Bennet, John, 81
Berdyaev, Nicholas, 167
Bible, 53ff, 66, 69, 71f, 73
Bixler, J.S., 118
Bosanquet, Bernard, 7
Bowne, Borden Parker, 4
Bradley, F.H., 7
Brightman, E.S., 51, 55, 153,
    177
Brown, Arlo Ares, 60
Brown, William Adams, 30
Brunner, Emil, 70, 117ff, 122

C

Calvin, John, 68
Cauthen, Kenneth, 1, 29, 51
Cherry, Clinton, 74
Craig, S.G., 29
Curtis, Olin, 10, 32f, 119f,
    139
Cushman, Ralph, 67

D

Davis, George W., 118
Death of Christ, 18f, 163f
Divinity of Christ, 15, 26f,
    38, 39, 93ff, 122
Dostoievsky, Fyodor, 68

E

Erasmus, 2
Experience, 3, 56, 64

F

Faulkner, John A., 11
Ferre, Nels, 152, 167
Fosdick, Harry Emerson,
    1, 30, 34, 81

G

Garvie, A.M., 122
Greeves, Frederic, 154

H

Hardwick, Charlie, 70,
    152, 154, 174, 175
Harmon, Nolan, 74
Hawk, Jonathan B., 75
Hegel, G.W.F., 13, 99
Hocking, W.E., 59, 60, 64
Homrighausen, Elmar, 78, 81
Horton, Douglas, 80
Horton, Walter Marshall,
    52, 78, 82
Hough, Lynn Harold, 78
Humanity of Christ, 15,
    27f, 102f, 108
Hutchinson, William, 79

I

Immanence, 4, 7, 30, 68
Incarnation, 10, 25f, 39,
    96f, 108f, 117, 119,
    122, 124, 161f

J

Jones, S. Jameson, 78, 173